LETTERS THAT MOVED MY FATHER

a memoir

ROMAYNE KAZMER

AQUARIUS PRESS
DETROIT, MICHIGAN

Letters That Moved My Father

Cover art: Courtesy of Romayne Kazmer
Books photos: Courtesy of Romayne Kazmer

ISBN 978-1-7357408-0-5
Library of Congress Control Number: 2020913677

Aquarius Press LLC
www.AquariusPress.net

Printed in the United States of America

DEDICATION

This book is dedicated to my father, Peter Troost, who was so moved by the letters I wrote home from my year abroad that he saved them in his safety deposit box. That is where they were found when he died in 1970.

It is also dedicated to my mother, Romaine Troost, who gave me the confidence that I could do anything that I choose. So when I was 23 years old I went around the world by myself, but that is another story.

Table of Contents

INTRODUCTION

Having just finished reading Bill Clinton's book wherein he says that everyone has a story, I realize I too have a story. The story I am going to tell you is the year that changed my life. It is the year I can recount to you because my father saved all the letters I wrote home from my year studying abroad in Switzerland and Norway. My father was a hard working successful businessman and not the type to show much emotion over the normal events of my life but these letters touched him. After I returned home his friends would relate to me the events that I had experienced in Europe as told to them by my father. When he died my letters were found in his safety deposit box.

Where do I begin? In 1959 as a sophomore at the University of Colorado, I was home in Glen Ellyn, Illinois for Christmas break. During this vacation, while in the shoe department in Marshall Fields in Oak Park, Illinois, I met some nuns from Rosary College nearby. Rosary College was one of the few schools that had student exchange programs in Europe at that time. They told me about their program abroad for college students. I was fascinated by the program and wanted to go. Where did this decision come from I do not know. Neither of my parents, relatives or friends had ever been to Europe at that time or was planning to go. I grew up in a typical Midwestern town where I was unaware of racial or ethnic differences. To me people were all pretty much the same. Through political connections of my mother's I was able to find a space in this program. I was destined to go.

I was accepted into Rosary College Junior Year Abroad program. The fall of 1959 I sailed from the west side pier in New York City on the SS Ryndam, Holland American Cruise Line for Cobb, Ireland. Friends from my hometown went to see me off in New

York. Immediately upon boarding the SS Ryndam a girl in my new program, from a large Irish family befriended me and included me in her farewell party onboard.

The girl from the little Midwestern suburb was overwhelmed with joy and happiness as I made my way across the Atlantic Ocean with my new classmates and chaperoning nuns. I left behind a world I knew to face one I would soon learn to love and would never again be the same small town girl. A giant world had opened up to me. I loved it and absorbed it like a sponge.

The following letters follow my journey from being that small Midwestern girl to becoming a citizen of the world. They reflect the times and morals of the late 50's and early 60's. But most of all they show my great love and fascination for the European and Middle Eastern peoples and their life styles.

I have never been the same person since I sailed across the ocean that fall day in 1959. My first letter home on September 15, 1959 shows my enthusiasm and life at that time.

Chapter 1

Leaving the United States for Europe

September 15, 1959

LETTERS FROM EUROPE—ROMAYNE'S YEAR ABROAD

1959-1960

Tuesday, September 15, 1959

(on Holland America Line stationery)

Dear Mom and Dad, you may be surprised but not only did I make it aboard this ship but my purse, camera, two suitcases, and trunk are also with me! Yah!!

I had a great time the few days I spent in New York. Linda Kemp (friend from Colo. Univ.) met us at the station and showed us around while we were there. Also, saw my old boyfriend Brian (from C.U.)!!!! Ann Pruitt (another friend from C.U.) came down from Briarcliff Manor and had lunch with me before I left. We all had a gay time! Even went to Coney Island. Fun.

When I came aboard the ship the photographer took my picture for the *Glen Ellyn News, Daily Journal,* and *Du Page Press*—please watch for it and send it to me. Also, would like to receive the Glen Ellyn News at school.

Went to a Bon Voyage party in Pat's cabin. (She's with my group.) She comes from a tremendous Irish family. Her two brothers, sister, and folks were there with the rest of her friends. Fun! Fun! Fun!!!

The next morning I received the beautiful orchid you sent!! I was so happy I could have cried for everyone else had received flowers, telegrams, or candy but me. Thank you so very much for it was just what I needed to make my trip complete. I am only sorry I didn't know this was the custom when you went to Europe.

The food is delicious!! We must have at least nine courses at every meal. Great for the diet! I eat at a big table for about 20 and sit with a nun who is really terrific. She was telling me about a little boy aboard ship who saw her cross and said "Too bad about Him". She said, "Yes, it was really mean."

See Meg on ship every day, so I never have a dull moment. When they don't have something planned like movies, bingo, horse races, dancing, etc. we hunt up something fun to do.

I met three Dutch sailors aboard ship who are going back to Amsterdam as passengers. They promised to show me around when I arrive there. Don't worry they are all safe. They told me that our last name is Dutch and is a name of a pipe tobacco in Holland!! The other fellows aboard ship are "drips" for the most part, in my opinion. I have played Checkers with my Dutch friends and their way is different and more difficult than ours.

The weather for the first two days was nice; however, lately it is always cloudy and chilly. Prices aboard ship are really cheap 10 cents for a Heineken Dutch beer, 40 cents gin and tonic, $1.00 for a haircut, 40 cents for a hair wash, 10 cents for a coke, 18 cents for a pack of filter tip cigarettes.

THE DAILY JOURNAL Page 8—Wed., Sept. 18, 19[illegible]

MISS ROMAYNE TROOST of 637 Lake Road, Glen Ellyn, is shown as she posed on the Holland-America Liner Ryndam, just before sailing from New York for the junior year abroad program of Rosary College.
(Photo courtesy of the Holland-America Line)

Romayne is seated in the back left.

Thursday 1:15AM

Hi again!

Well, there are many more things to write about but it is very late and I must get off today at 7:00 A.M. I'm very tired for typical of me I have been staying up very, very late but having a tremendous time!

I feel I am very fortunate to be here and soon in Fribourg after Ireland, England, Paris, Brussels, Amsterdam, Cologne, Heidelberg. For already I think this year will probably be one of the most wonderful years of my life thanks to both of you.

I have a cold—just finished a hot lemonade so I must go to sleep now. Love and good-night,
Romayne

P.S. Bud, Dick, Frank, Susie – Hello to all and please write me!

P.S.S. "Hi" to Fannie. (Note: She was our cleaning lady.)

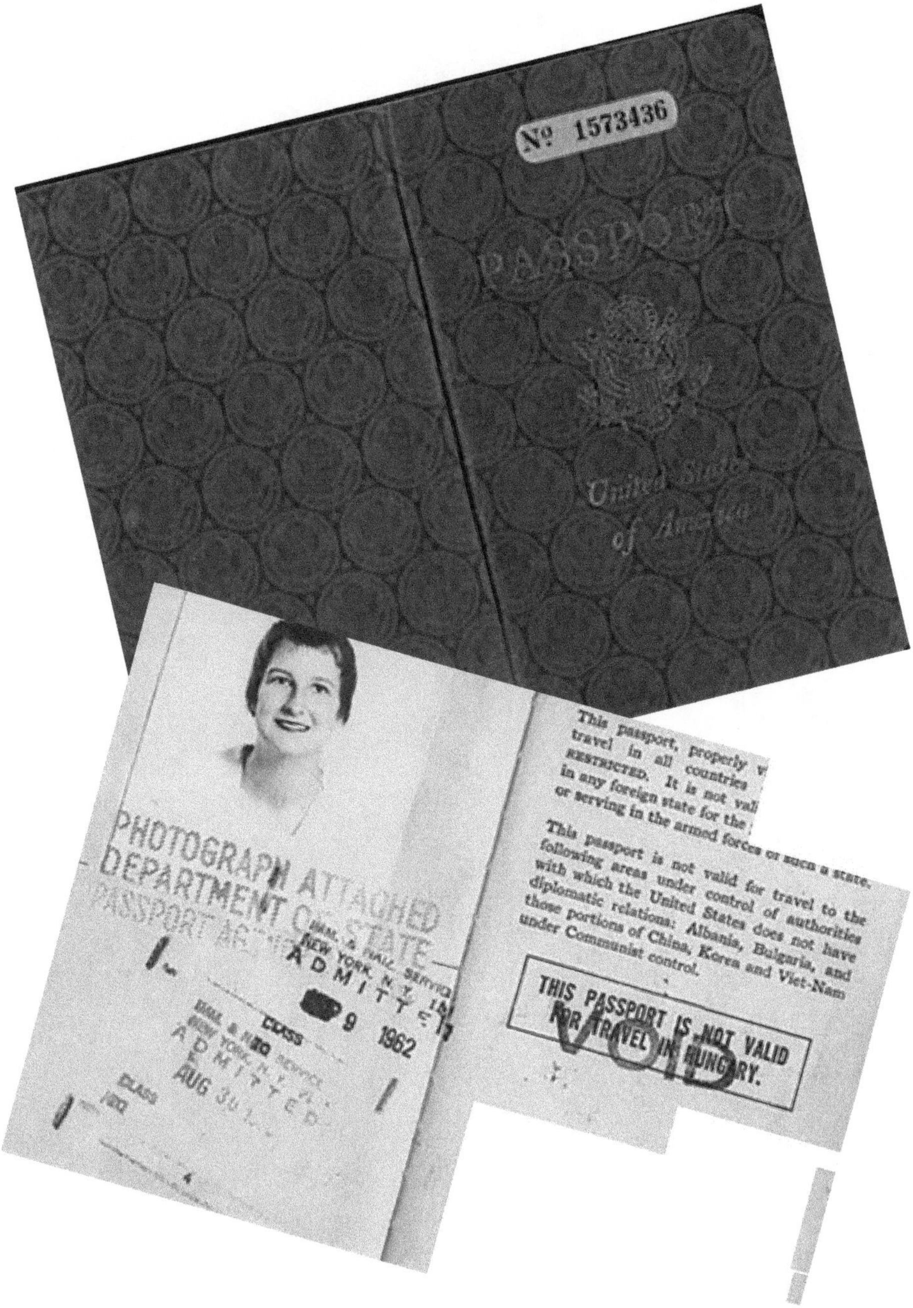

№ 1573436
PHOTOGRAPH ATTACHED
DEPARTMENT OF STATE
ADMITTED
1962
This passport, properly v
travel in all countries
RESTRICTED. It is not val
in any foreign state for the
or serving in the armed forces of such a state.
This passport is not valid for travel to the
following areas under control of authorities
with which the United States does not have
diplomatic relations: Albania, Bulgaria, and
those portions of China, Korea and Viet-Nam
under Communist control.
THIS PASSPORT IS NOT VALID
FOR TRAVEL IN HUNGARY.
VOID

Chapter 2

Impressions of Europe in Route to the Villa

September 21, 1959

Dublin
September 21, 1959

Hi Folks! Been having a tremendous time. Met a German fellow at an Irish dance last night who is going to show me around Heidelberg when I arrive. This morning he brought me a bon voyage card and a record of Irish songs!!

The sisters have been great. Hours have been 12:00 except for special things. Last night we didn't have to come in until 1:00 A.M. because of the dance. They give us a lot of freedom.

Tonight we fly to London then Paris, Brussels, Amsterdam, Cologne, Heidelberg, and then to the Villa!!!

Saw an Irish play in Killarney which was terrific. Also, took a ride in a jaunting car (sent a picture of one to Susie on a postcard.)

Food has been the same mashed potatoes all the time lamb, peas, or chicken and bacon, no salads, desserts are okay. Generally the food is fair.

Music here is mostly American. Haven't been able to find any leprechauns as yet! Actually I haven't even seen any shamrocks, because their season is only in the spring and summer.
Hope to go to "High Tea" now 5:45 P.M.

Love to all,
Romayne

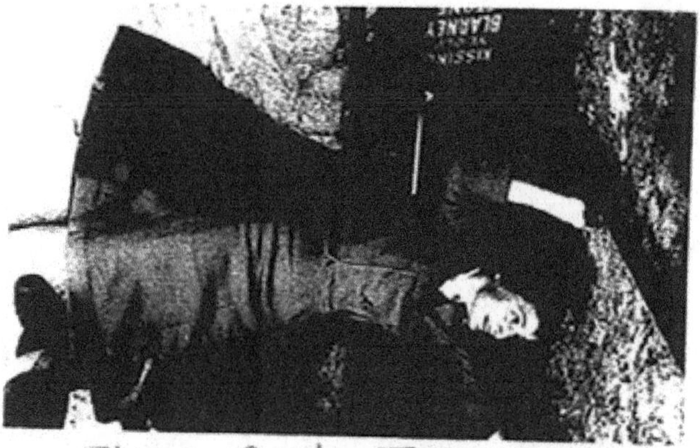

Blarney Castle, Ireland

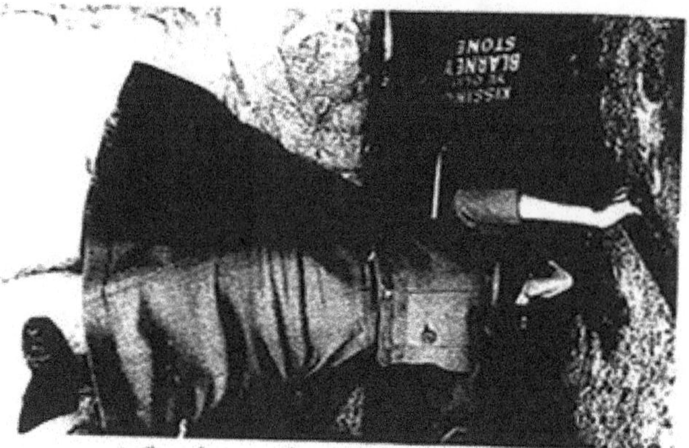

Kissing the Blarney Stone

Blarney Castle

Paris
September 30, 1959

Dear Mom and Dad,

London was not very gay, but very historical. It was really great to see all the things I have read and studied about for so long in school -- Shakespeare country, Canterbury etc. We even went to the Shakespeare Memorial Theater in Stratford on Avon and saw King Lear with Charles Laughton.

I had a seat in the fifth row center!

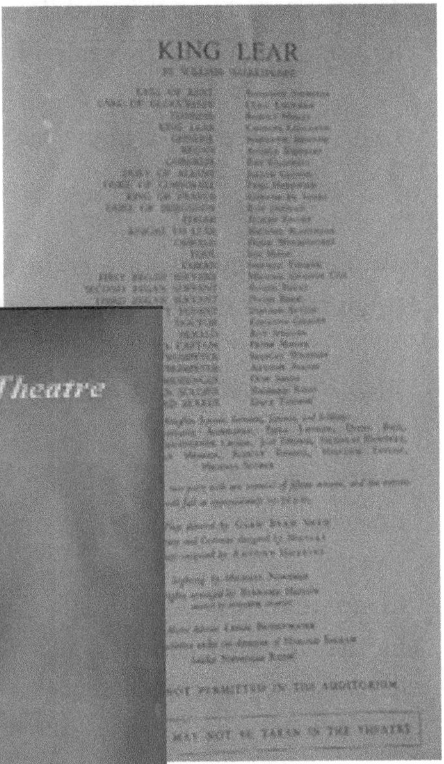
KING LEAR

Paris is a gay fun place!!!! Tonight four of us went to the Follies Bergeres. Today after our morning tour, Sue and I went to the top of the Eiffel Tower and then to the aristocratic section of Paris where the famous designers such as Christian Dior have their studios and shops. Naturally we walked into his studio showrooms. Really sharp—it was even perfumed. Then we went into a beauty salon and got French hairstyles in this section. It only cost me $1.15 for a wash and style. Looks like this: (sketch in letter)

The part starts in the middle and slants way to the side. Doesn't look as good as my drawing – but it's fun and gay.

Last night we took a night boat ride for two hours down Le Seine River. Beautiful!

Tomorrow night we are going to a place where they dance in the cellars. Don't worry I'm careful.

Also dressed up one night in short skirts, much eye makeup, berets, and sweaters and went to an outdoor café for drinks. Send you a picture of outfits later.

Romayne is wearing the beret.

The food in Paris is great. And, I love the outdoor cafes.

Fun! Fun! Fun!

Mom, I was really good to receive your letters for everyone in my group gets mail—even me now. Yes, my trunk was one of the last ones to arrive. I did take many of my cold pills, but colds are going around the group so it is hard to get rid of one—especially in cold damp Ireland. My ankle was really swollen on the boat. However, I slept with it elevated and it went back to almost normal. It still is a little swollen. There were so many flowers on the ship they didn't have time to deliver them all the night we left.

I have another suggestion for a maid. Call Mrs. Allen #GE1699 (Stewart's mother). She has a white woman. Since you are going to school, it may be a good idea to have her come in on Tues. and Thurs. to clean and cook a big dinner since you have much homework. Tell Fannie you decided to have this lady because she also cooks. Please let me know how this works out. Dad or Bud why don't you call Mrs. Allen if Mom doesn't have time.

As far as my major is concerned, what do you think about public relations instead of international relations? In a way I feel I would be more suited to this because I have always been able to make friends and organize things to do. On the ship I read about a lady in the field who worked for one of the big hotel chains and ran their affairs. I don't know if this is exactly what I want, but in a way I feel I am more qualified for this than international relations. What do you think? Do you have any idea of bigger jobs open to people in public relations? Mom and Dad, this major of mine is really a problem.

I would appreciate some advice on it before I have to sign up for classes about October 10. I am still interested in International Law. Mom, if you have time please ask an advisor at Elmhurst College just what would International Law involve etc. I suppose I will minor in French since most of my classes will be French and I don't want to go to school forever.

I can understand the Parisian French a little when the people speak very slowly.

Love,
Romayne

Hello to Bud, Frank, and Susie

I am fourth from right, second row

Chapter 3

School and Student Life at the Villa des Fougeres

October 18, 1959

Villa des Fougeres, Fribourg, Suisse (stationery)
October 18, 1959 Sunday

Dear Mom and Dad, I finally arrived last Sunday. The nuns had all the rooms ready with flowers, beds made, and a prayer book in French for each of us. The apartment room I live in is really nice. Everything is new and is much better living here than in the Villa because I can get away from "the eyes of the nuns." However, everything is very strict. Six pages of rules restrict me from most all fun things. However, it is not too bad since the town is rather dead anyway. The Swiss fellows on the whole look rather "seedy". Shock – we can have beer in our apartment refrigerator. Friday night we had a party with the Georgetown fellows (Americans studying here) in the Villa parlor. The nuns were good about the party, they allowed beer and didn't complain about the noise.

Mom, I haven't received the mail you forwarded to me as yet. I think it is really great you are graduating!! Please send me an announcement. I'm sorry I won't be there to see you graduate. Dad should be really proud.

Dad, I would appreciate it if you would write Sister Benvenuta directly and tell her I have your permission to go swimming, boating, horseback riding and skiing. Otherwise, I can't do any of these things. Also, include that I'm a proficient skier and have already taken skiing lessons.

Please add that I may participate in any sport. Dad, I would appreciate it if you would send me a copy of the letter you write to Sister Benvenuta.

The inside lens in my camera came loose in Germany. So I don't have any pictures of Germany. My camera guarantee is in my right hand top desk drawer, please send it to me. A man in a German camera shop said maybe it was because of the weather.

I didn't have much choice about my schedule since the only classes I could take were French classes, and three English classes, and one class in Theology. Therefore, I am taking 17 ½ credits with 24 hours of class per week. Somehow I have 16 classes!!!! Only one class carries 3 credits per semester. The rest are either 2, 1, or ½ credits per semester. Have pity on me at final time with 16 tests. University classes start Wednesday.

All the girls here except five have been going to Catholic girls schools. They have been so pampered and restricted, I don't know how some of them will ever be independent or get along by themselves after they get out of school. Yet, they are real nice girls.

My roommate, Nannette Ladwig, from Elmhurst, went to the University of Wisconsin. She has a lot more "on the ball" than most of these girls.

The food here is delicious. The sister in charge is a tremendous cook. However, the meals are very frustrating because we have to speak in French.

Reactions to the rest of the trip before arriving are as follows. Didn't like Brussels, liked Amsterdam took a canal boat ride and saw old Holland where they still dress in native outfits, (also saw my friend I met on the ship). Cologne was extremely modern because everything was bombed during the war. I really liked Heidelberg. It is beautiful. Also, many fun places such as The Red Ox Inn, Sippets, and the Cave to go at night. All the students go to these places and they sing real German drinking songs.

The hours here are 12:15 Friday and Saturday and 8:45 weekdays except one night a week we can stay out until 11:15. I think 8:45 is ridiculous. Students should have later hours for it should be up to them to study if they go to college.

Love, Romayne

Patty Belton in front, Me in the air (back)

My roommate, Nannette

October 22, 1959

Dear Mom and Dad,

Well, classes have finally started! I'm having a horrible time understanding them in French. Every night I have to go to the library to find a book with today's lecture and then translate it into English and take my notes from there. If you have time and find a lightweight 17th century French literature book I would appreciate it if you would send it to me airmail. Besides, you can send books real cheap through the mail.

Everything is expensive here including paper (50 cents for 15 cents worth), pens, ink 25 cents, etc.

I have been thinking over what I want for Christmas and since I have most everything, the thing I would really like is a big 8" by 10" colored and framed picture of both of you together. Please call up and make the appointment right away, so I can have it by Christmas.

My social life is still completely dead (worse than ever) because most of the men at the university are in the seminary!! Nanette knows quite a few people in Suisse, so please sign the enclosed letter and mail it directly to Sister Benvenuta immediately so I can go with her to visit them. She doesn't want to go by herself, so don't worry I am not intruding.

Please enclose a few bobby pins in each letter because they are 6 for 15 cents here and I'm letting my hair grow and will need them. Also, enclose some Gillette razor blades. Thanks.

Love, Romayne

P. S. Please send my camera guarantee immediately. If you can't find it, see if you can find the one for the other camera.

Dad, travelers checks are rather hard to get so I think maybe I should save the rest of mine for Xmas travels. If you think this is best please send me some more money. Otherwise, I have enough for a while.

By the way, I forgot to tell you I had fleas in Ireland!!!! I must have had at least 30 itchy bites. They haven't completely gone away yet. Sister B said they were common in Europe, and not to worry. They aren't like dog's fleas.

If you see Aunt Florence, by chance, ask her about Sister Meredith who is supposed to be related to us distantly. She is living here at the Villa and doesn't know how we are related. Ask Aunt Florence for further details please.

(Letter in same envelope to Sister Benvenuta giving permission to visit a list of friends of Dr. and Mrs. Ladwigs.)

Villa des Fougeres, Fribourg, Suisse
November 7, 1959

Dear Mom and Dad,

Since my last letter, I have been working hard at my school and getting my social life to function again. As far as school is concerned, I still can't understand the teachers very well and in my French Literature class I can't understand him at all. However, I am really working at it because I sit in the front row in almost every class so I can hear the teacher better. None of my good friends will sit with me because the profs always call on whoever sits in front! I would still appreciate it if you would send me immediately an airmail Literature of the 17th and 18th century book, because I understand we can take the final test in English in that class. And by the time I catch on to the French lectures I am going to be way behind. The profs here are a real riot! Each one is distinctly an individual with either long hair, funny beard, or bald with a long beard. You would have to see them to really appreciate them.

My social life has really picked up. Last night I had a date with a German fellow, quite harmless, I met at Georgetown Halloween Party. We went down to the old part of Fribourg called the Bas Ville and into a "moldy" bar where all the local color goes. I can't quite describe it, but took movies in a bar similar the week before on a Sunday afternoon, which I shall send home as soon as I have time. Also, have a date to go ice- skating with a Swiss fellow, real cute, next Friday. The American fellows here are "so so" but I can't see any sense in coming to Europe to just date Americans when you can do that in the States.

Went to the show last week in English. It was really great. The first show Fribourg has had in English so far. However, it was an old FBI movie back to the days when people still wore double-breasted suits. The thing, which really aggravated me, though was at the beginning they said three out of every four people in the city would be killed by a murder. I think this is a terrible impression to give Europeans. But, the most thrilling part of the movie was the newsreel. It was a great feeling when they would show Brussels, the Arc de Triumph in Paris, and other spots, which I had actually seen myself.

By the way, I am using this typewriter instead of mine because on the way over something happened to mine and the capital letters are raised above the small letters when I type.

Another sport which I have taken up again from my White Lake Days is Hitch-hiking or as they call it over here auto-stopping. I am convinced it is the way to see Switzerland and really meet the people. Besides since they only speak French it also helps me with my comprehension and ability to speak French. So far we, Nannette, Susie, (from Riverside, Ill.) and myself, have gone to Bern, La Roche, and Lausanne this way. The people are really tremendous and very friendly to us. Mom, I even asked a Swiss fellow how people reacted to girls' hitch-hiking and he said it was perfectly acceptable.

Had a neat time in LaRoche, a podunk junction town. Auto-stopped out there with Nannette and two fellows from Georgetown. We went in the old country hotel bar where just about the whole town goes on Sunday and had a liter of wine. There were a group of fellows there singing drinking songs in French they even sang "Tom Dooley" in French!!!!

We haven't had much snow as yet, but it sure is cold. Our apartment is not really cold now. But, at first we froze because the heat wasn't on full blast and they didn't have the downstairs front door on until yesterday. All the cold air came in every time we opened our apartment door.

Dad, I really appreciate your offering to buy me an electric blanket, but would appreciate it if someone would send me my white sweater. I am almost finished knitting with my ball of white yarn, size 15 and 8 needles and knitting directions. I would like to finish it and wear it for it is a bulky sweater. It is in the box where I had my winter clothes stored. It may still be in the hall or laundry room. Mom, you know the box where you put some of your clothes and Susie's clothes too. Also, if you will send me my knitting book, which is in my headboard, and the size needles that sweater I promised to knit for you, I will whip it up over here. All my needles are in my headboard. If the knitting book isn't in my headboard, it is in the section just above my drawers. By the way, my knitting may be in the fourth or fifth drawer down.

I would appreciate it if you would let me know what to buy you for Christmas. Since I didn't see all the things you bought over here, I have no idea of what you have and don't have. Please let me know right away so I can get it in the mail on time. Susie also.

Susie, did you ever get the birthday present I mailed to you from Heidelberg? And, how did you like it? Please write and tell me all about your birthday party and the other presents you got.

Also, how was Halloween? What costume did you wear? They don't celebrate Halloween over here. Susie, it is really terrible no one has a pumpkin and the kids don't even go trick or treating.

The skirt styles over here are just at knee level. All my skirts are too long. One of them now has a five-inch hem. I am afraid to cut them off in case the hemlines come down again. My camelhair coat is so long it looks like I'm drowning in it!

Two weeks ago on Sunday, Nannette and I went down to Luzern by train to meet these friends of her aunt's friend. It was really gay. The man's two sons met us at the train and we all went to church together. Then we went to their house and had lunch, which consisted of chicken, French fries, peas, and wine with grapes for desert. They were a typical Swiss family and lived in a little chalet on the lake there. The father took us to the plant where he works and showed us around.

Since he makes calendars and similar products, he gave us a beautiful Swiss calendar and a little notebook. Then his sons took us to Lichtenstein up in the mountains. We took the trip up one of them in the sky train. Stopped and had pastry and took the night train back. Saw Buchers where you all bought watches but it was closed. Definitely agree with you Mom about Luzern being the prettiest town in all of Switzerland.

Dad, I don't know if you have paid for the Christmas trip yet. It is $180. and is due December 5. They haven't said anything about the spring trip yet except we go back to Paris for a week and spend 3 days in a convent after we see Italy. I am not" gung-ho" to go back to Paris or spend 3 days in a convent until I see the rest of Europe. I am trying to work something else out. The Christmas trip will really be fun. We go skiing at Zermatt for 4 days, then to Vienna, Salzburg, and Munich. Meg probably won't be in Vienna when I am there. Since I will be there for New Year's Eve, I am going to try to have her line some dates up for some of us.

Please don't forget to enclose bobby pins, razor blades, and stretch nylons in the letters you write to me. I bought some nylons in England and they are terrible. They never stay up!! Stretch nylons like you bought me for my birthday is exactly what I need for I am sure they will fit. Still waiting for all the mail you forwarded to me,

Mom. Did the earrings I ordered from Macy's ever come? Dad loved your letters. Hope to hear from you all soon.
Love, Romayne

Villa des Fougeres Fribourg, Suisse
November 19, 1959 Friday

Dear Mom and Dad,

I have really been having a "blast." Wednesday we didn't have school because the University finally got around to celebrating the beginning of the term. At night all the fraternities had a torch light procession (just for men), but Nannette and I marched with the lead group because we met the officers on the way to the start of the procession. We marched all the way through town to a square where we all threw in our torches and had a bonfire. Fraternities over here are just for men. The different ones wear different hats and colors across their chests to class. Then since we were in the lead fraternity we had to march around the bonfire and to the café where the fraternity always meets. We sang tons of songs in French that I have no idea of what they mean much less what the words were. Then they made us get up and sing an American song. We sang Tom Dooley and they sang some song about America back to us in French. Every Friday night for ten weeks we go to dancing lessons with the candidates for the fraternity and then at a huge formal ball we get our colors. No other girls are in the fraternities, that I know of, so this is really a big honor!!!! Forgot, we become members for life.

Have to run to class now --- will finish this letter later......

Nov. 25, 1959
Wednesday

I'm sick in bed tonight have the stomach flu. It has been going around here and I'm one of the last to catch it. Feel better now though because I just "gave up all the food on my stomach."

Tomorrow is Thanksgiving and all Americans are excused from classes! Our cook is preparing a huge turkey dinner for us. There is also a big party planned for all Americans at the Hotel Fribourg. Mom received your letter, thanks much for the money for Thanksgiving. Hope everybody at home has a nick Thanksgiving. Say "hello" to Jack Gunnell for me.

The only thing I am really worried about is my mail. This really upsets me because by the time I receive it I probably won't have any friends left. Mom, if you don't have time to send it please give it to Dad to take to the office and have his secretary sent it airmail to me immediately.

Dad I received your money thanks. I had the darndest time getting it in Travelers Checks like you specified because the bank thought they should keep it for me. However, it is all settled now and I'm sending you the receipt.

It you ever send me anything be sure to mark on the customs sticker under $10.00 gift regardless of the price and I will too so we won't ever have to pay customs duties.

Susie and I went to our first dancing lessons last Friday. It was a riot! There were three other Swiss girls there. We learned the tango in French to some "offbeat" music!!

Went skiing at Villar for the weekend two weeks ago! It was too early in the season to rent skis, but one of the girls that went with me got sick and went home so I used her equipment. The only tow that was open was on the advanced slope (I have never been off the beginners slope), which I didn't know until the end of the day. The only tow was a rope tow and the man at the bottom didn't speak English—I have never been on a tow like this before!! It only stopped three times all day—one for lunch and twice for me. The first time I fell off and the second time I was dragged up because my feet slipped off the path and I fell over!

How was the "get together" for Senator Humphrey? Who was all there?

Enclosing a clipping from the Glen Ellyn News, which may help matters at home. If this lady is already taken, maybe she will know of someone else for you.

Don't really need an electric blanket, because it is warm now. If you really want to send me some money some skis and boots would be nice. Also a transistor radio or watch.

Some of the kids have them and can get the Armed Forces program from Luxembourg with all the latest news and songs from America. Please let me know when you receive my five rolls of film and Christmas package. It is rather difficult to buy anything typically Swiss now because the tourist season is over—I couldn't even get any Swiss cards like yours, Mom.

Dad, I still have five rolls of film. When I need more I will let you know. When you send some more film, please enclose a couple of rolls for night pictures.

Susie, still waiting for a letter from you. It's your turn to write. How did you like your birthday present? If you had pictures taken at school again this year, how about sending me one?

That's about all for now. Please don't forget my mail. Frank, hope you had a Happy Birthday. Say "hello" to the boys and Susie for me. Love, Romayne

P.S. The battery in my radio is still good if anybody wants to use a portable. Also, in you next letter please enclose my charm bracelet in my top drawer of my dresser. It's silver and has only three charms on it.

Got a permanent here for only $8.75! It really looks good and isn't "frizzy" at all. Really looks natural, yet my hair really has body now. First permanent I have really been happy with. Don't even have to set it, except when I wash it. Hairdressers are cheap here only $1.75 for a wash and set at one the best shops.

Villa des Fougeres Fribourg, Suisse
Dec. 10, 1959

Dear Mom and Dad,

Well, first of all congratulations to Mom for running for Congress! Win or lose it is a great honor just to be considered worthy enough to be put up to run. Mom, I'm very proud of you and if there is anything I can do way over here just let me know. I would love to see the DuPage Press where you made headlines if you have an extra copy.

Dad was good to receive your letter and hear all is going well at home. Promise to look into a Mercedes Benz when I get to Germany. The money for the Christmas trip $180 has to be in right now. Do you want me to pay Sister Benvenuta for it in Travelers Checks or are you going to send me a check for it? I am enclosing an article for another cleaning lady just in case the one we now have doesn't work out.

Have been thinking about going to the University of Oslo, Norway, for summer school. It is all taught in English. I think maybe I can even get credit towards my major. Since I will probably have to go to summer school anyway to graduate, I am going to try to get a scholarship to go to Oslo. What do you think of this idea?

One of the girls who lives with me in the apartments is from Tehran, Iran. She has invited some of us to spend part of spring vacation at her house. She is a Moslem and her father is some "big wheel" in the army. We thought perhaps we would go as far as Italy with the group. Then leave them when they go through France and back to Paris since we have already been there. If we could take this cut off at Italy for the same price of the spring trip so it would cost you the same amount, would you give me permission to go to Tehran from Italy? I haven't gotten all the details and prices of transportation worked out now, but will let you know my exact plans when everything is planned out smoothly.

Vida is a real nice girl and has been going to college in the States for the past two years.

My fraternity dancing lessons are really a riot! Instead of learning one, two, three, we learn to dance un, deux, trios. All my "fraternity brothers" are real nice fellows, even though all the new members can't dance! All the older members come to the lessons later in the evening. Last week we did the Vienna Waltz.

My Christmas addresses and schedule are as follows:

Dec. 22-26 Hotel Gornergrat, Zermatt, Switzerland
Dec. 27 on the train
Dec. 28-Jan.1 Hotel Regina, Rooseveltplatz 15, Vienna, Austria
Jan. 2-3 Hotel Pitter, Salzburg, Germany
Jan. 4 Hotel Schottenhamel, Munich, Germany
Jan. 5 Train to Fribourg

Since Tuesday was the feast of the Immaculate Conception, we didn't have school all day. We get off on all holy days. Four of us hitch hiked to Geneva for the day. Met a interesting man on the way who builds most of the ski lifts in Switzerland. He was going to take us all with him to inspect different tows but we had to be back in Fribourg before dark. Got one ride as far as Lausanne and then we had to split up to get a ride back. Got two rides and then had to take the train the last 12 miles because we couldn't get another ride!! Geneva was interesting. I think it is a good place to have "peace talks". With the big lake there and the swans it is very pretty. Went to the American Express there to get information on our trip to Iran.

Saw the Diary of Anne Frank at the movies in French. It was very good. If you want to see a good movie, I advise you all to go. My friend from Holland thought it was excellent because they pronounce all the names of people and towns the Dutch way and not the American way. The story takes place in Amsterdam during the war. It is really thrilling to see Amsterdam with its canals and all and to think that I have seen all this for myself in person. By the way, have you received the rolls of film I sent home as yet?

My Dutch friend is on the roll I took on the boat "Ryndam."
My darn camera is broken again. I was all set to take some pictures of the Saint Nicholas parade Dec. 6 and the roll sounded like it was out of film. But, I just put a new roll of film in the camera. It didn't even sound like there was any film in the camera. I checked the roll and it was put in correctly.

The parade was really great! All the little "brats" in the whole town were there. Saint Nicholas rode through the town on a donkey and following him were two men all dressed in black with switches to hit the bad boys and girls. Then Saint Nicholas had helpers to throw cookie in shapes of Santa Clauses etc. to the good "kids". This parade went down to the old Cathedral in the Bas Ville where Saint Nicholas got up on the balcony of the church and made a speech. The funny part was after the speech the whole town has a confetti fight. There are stands selling confetti and everyone in the town throws it at each other!! Everyone is full of tiny bits of paper from head to foot. P.S. No, I didn't get switched, I got a cookie.

Funniest thing yet was last night. We all had to be in bed by 9:30. Then we were all given Hot Toddys made with brandy to fight our colds and sickness. We were supposed to go right to bed to sweat!

Last time I wrote I was sick in bed. Well instead of being well the next day like I planned I had to stay in bed five days! It was miserable everybody was running around and having a blast but me. The medicine they have over here is terrible. It isn't flavored like they have in the States and tastes horrible.

I'm happy to hear you are going to send me a watch so I can wear all the bands I brought with me. Don't forget it is the square one I want. Also, I will love the ski boots for with my long narrow feet I have a horrible time renting a pair of boots that fit properly.

However, don't forget the thing I really want is the picture I asked for. Everyone thinks all the bands are really "neat"!

Will try to arrange a call home Christmas. However, I understand sometimes it takes five hours to get a line through so if it is a little late I can't help it. Should I call person to person? Will you be at Aunt Bernice's or at home?

Not too much else is now....write soon. Almost forgot, Mother do I have mail at home or not? You wrote and said I did and Dad wrote and said there is none to forward to me.
Very important!!!!

Love, Ro

P.S. Received the book you sent me from K&B's. It is a big help because it has sort of a short summary on authors of the 17th century and helps me put the notes I take in class together. For sometimes I just get a name and have no idea of their connection to his lecture. Never dreamed it would be so expensive to send. Thanks, Mom. Don't worry, I am really using it. Haven't received the other book you sent as yet. Tell Bud and Susie I am still waiting to hear from them!

P.P.S. Had my camera fixed here because it only cost $3.00 and decided that I would probably have to pay that much for postage back to the States. The man sent it to Zurich to have it fixed. Revere doesn't have a factory here in Switzerland. However, I am going to send the bill with my guarantee to the Revere representative in Zurich to see if I can get my money back. Would have had to send it airmail to the State with insurance on it.

Chapter 4

Christmas Away from Home

December 26, 1959

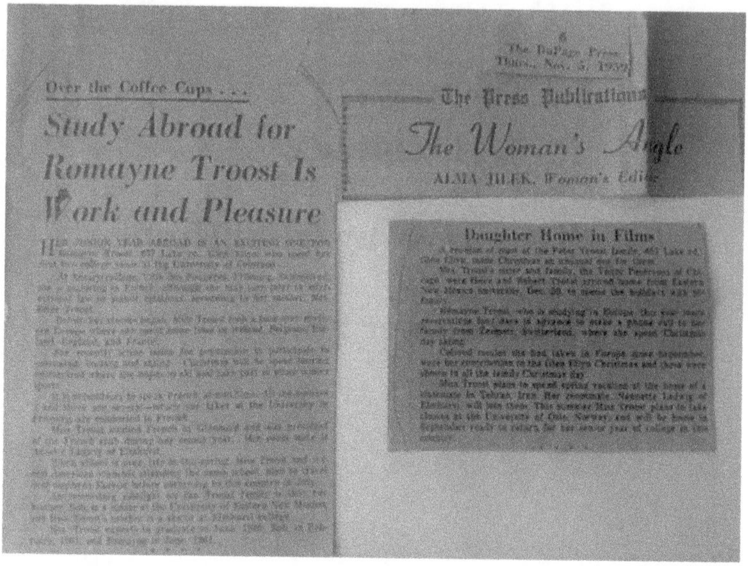

The DuPage Press
Thurs., Nov. 5, 1959

The Press Publications

The Woman's Angle

ALMA JILEK, Woman's Editor

Over the Coffee Cups . . .

Study Abroad for Romayne Troost Is Work and Pleasure

Daughter Home in Films

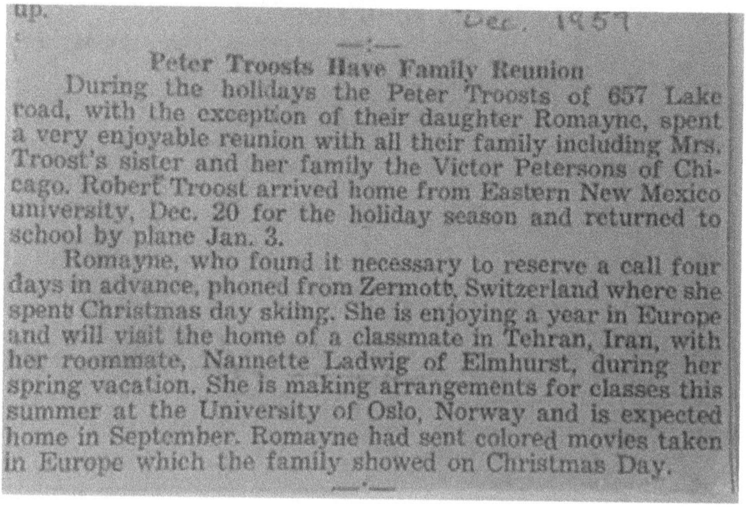

Dec. 1959

Peter Troosts Have Family Reunion

During the holidays the Peter Troosts of 657 Lake road, with the exception of their daughter Romayne, spent a very enjoyable reunion with all their family including Mrs. Troost's sister and her family the Victor Petersons of Chicago. Robert Troost arrived home from Eastern New Mexico university, Dec. 20 for the holiday season and returned to school by plane Jan. 3.

Romayne, who found it necessary to reserve a call four days in advance, phoned from Zermott, Switzerland where she spent Christmas day skiing. She is enjoying a year in Europe and will visit the home of a classmate in Tehran, Iran, with her roommate, Nannette Ladwig of Elmhurst, during her spring vacation. She is making arrangements for classes this summer at the University of Oslo, Norway and is expected home in September. Romayne had sent colored movies taken in Europe which the family showed on Christmas Day.

The Matterhorn at Zermatt

Dec. 26, 1959

(note on back of card)

Dear Mom and Dad, it was really great to talk to both of you yesterday. It didn't really seem like Xmas until I heard your voices. I made the reservation for the call four days before Xmas.

This is a beautiful place to spend the holiday. It has been snowing and only way to get around is by sleigh! Skiing is fun. I'm having a wonderful time. Wish you were all here.

Love, Romayne

Hi gang!

Well, this is the first year we haven't all been together for Christmas. Sure seems strange being 3500 miles away now! I can just picture you Carol, Dick, and Bob coming down stairs in your "casual manner" while you Frank and Susie have been up for hours!! Of course, your Mom and Dad have Susie "pounding" on your door every few minutes to get up!

And, then there will be the huge, as always delicious, Xmas dinner Mother has "slaved over" for days. Susie, will be elected "chief bread butter upper" for the dressing, which nobody but Dad, Mom, and I still enjoy and I shall miss.

Then, of course, midnight mass which brings in the true spirit of Xmas.

NEW YEAR'S CARD
(Bonne et Heureuse Annee – inside card)

Hi Gang!

Well this is the first year we haven't been together for Christmas. Sure seems strange being 3500 miles away now! I can just picture you Bud, Dick, and Bob coming downstairs in your "casual manner" while Frank and Susie have been up for hours!! Of course, you Mom and Dad have been "pounced" on every few minutes to get up!

And, the then there will be the huge, as always delicious, Xmas dinner mother has "slaved over" for days. Susie will be elected "chief bread puller apart" for the dressing which nobody but Dad, Mom, will enjoy and I will miss.

Then of course, midnight mass that brings in the true spirit of Christmas.

Hope you all Mom, Dad, Bud, Dick, Bob, Frank and Susie have a very Merry Christmas!! Wish I could be there with you. However, they have a nice vacation planned for me. I will be in Zermatt skiing for Xmas, to Vienna for New Years, and home via Munich and Salzburg. But, Christmas away from home just won't be the same.

Love, Ro

Villa des Fougeres
Fribourg, Suisse
January 8, 1959

Dear Mom and Dad,

Received the picture of you two when I returned to Fribourg Wed. Thank you. It is really an excellent picture of both of you. I only hope you are as happy as you look in it!!!

Bought some excellent ski boots in Suisse, which should last me a lifetime. They cost $25. Also sent for the watch in Luzern. Thank you again for the presents. Did you receive the things I sent home yet? The lady in the store told me they should only take three weeks to reach the states regular mail. So therefore I sent them regular mail three weeks and a half before Christmas.

I am really sorry about my movies. Did the last roll I took of Fribourg turn out? I took that after I had the lens fixed. When I received your letter I had a new roll of film in the camera. I took it back to the camera store for the man to check and he said it seemed okay. He told me to take another roll and have him develop it so he could see what the matter was. Over my vacation I took another roll of film and will take it in to him this afternoon and let you know the outcome. I wrote to the Revere representative in Zurich about the guarantee on my camera and am enclosing letter he sent back to me.

Dad thanks much for finally forwarding my mail to me.

The Christmas vacation was wonderful! Zermatt was beautiful. It snowed much of the time and the skiing at the foot of the Matterhorn was a thrilling experience. We took a sleigh to midnight mass in the little town church, which was cold and crowded with people but a beautiful service. It was snowing Christmas Eve and Christmas Day. It was a beautiful Christmas and just like you would imagine it should be like with the snow, pine trees, mountains, sleigh bells, and the little church. I am sorry you all could not be there to enjoy it with me.

I met an old man on the slopes must be about 60 who was from England and skiing for the first time. He was a bulky man and was having a horrible time standing on his skis.

I tried to help him. He told me if I ever came to England again to visit him and his wife. They live six miles from the ocean, 20 miles from England, in a little town with an old Roman castle and wall. If some of the boys decide to go to Europe I will write this couple and I am sure they will be welcome to visit them. For it really helps to know someone to really show you around over here.

Zermatt over the holidays was full of English people. Almost everybody spoke English; however when we went to Vienna it was different everybody spoke German and nobody even knew French. Vienna was nice and we probably saw just about the same things you did while you were there, except I am sure it must have been nicer in the summer. New Year's Eve was fun!!! We had a cocktail party in our hotel to start things off. Some of the fellows from Georgetown were in Vienna at this time so we went out with them to some of the nightspots in Vienna. Also, hit a few "moldy" wine cellars in the basement of restaurants including one in the downstairs of the city hall! Mom, finally made it to the Opera, saw the Flying Dutchman by Wagner. Only fell asleep three times during the first act! The rest of the Opera I stayed awake. The costumes, voices, and scenes were beautiful, but since I didn't know the story behind it wasn't too interesting. Also saw the Vienna Boys Choir and Spanish Riding

Horses. Saw the Vienna Boys Choir at mass on New Year's Day. Obviously I was very tired, started to kneel down where the kneeler usually is but since it wasn't there I fell down on the floor!!!

Salzburg should definitely not be visited until summer. We took a tour of the city and everything was closed including boards over the fountains and statues on this tour! We couldn't see anything except the castle and that was closed because the funicular going up was run on waterpower and in the winter the water froze.

In Munich I hunted down the Mercedes Benz factory. They said it is impossible to get any Mercedes before March or April of 1961!! And, then you cannot order one from the factory unless someone will pick it up in Munich. To get one shipped to the States it is necessary to order it through a company in the States. If you think a member of the family will be in Munich in 1962, I can find out more information and order a car for you. Also, went to the Volkswagen Dealer. I can get a Volkswagen in May or June in a pretty green color with a sunroof and United States specifications for $1,200. The man said it would cost me $150 to ship it home plus customs. There is some way I can get around taxes by giving a Colorado address when I buy it. Right now I have about $1,200 in the bank, I would have to borrow some money from you Dad to get this car. How much are Volkswagens in the States? Do you think it is a good idea I get one over here? Would you loan me the remainder of the money I need until I start working? I have some savings bonds would someone please check and let me know how many I have. I have to order the car quickly and already have the order blank so please let me know if it is okay.

At night in Munich, five of us went out with three fellows from Jordan and two from Turkey!

Don't worry they were safe. One of the girls with us lives in Munich. They are friends of hers. The fellows from Jordan spoke English, but the Turks spoke French and German, and the girl from Munich spoke German and English. So all-night we would have to translate things for the rest of the group. We went to the Schwabing section of the city, which is like Greenwich Village in New York. Later two of the girl went home with the three fellows from Jordan and we met another friend of this girl who lives in Italy. It was a very interesting night we spent in all the little hangouts of this section of the city. And, now I am back in Fribourg where classes are starting off very slowly. I can't really tell you how I am doing in anything since we haven't had any exams in most of my classes. The only exam I have had was in Theology and I haven't gotten it back as yet; and a couple of quizzes in grammar which only one has come back and I got a 94.

Forgot to tell you, before I left for vacation we all took out a little orphan and gave her a pair of pajamas and a toy. We brought our orphans to the apartment were we had a French Xmas tree with candles and sparklers and gave them a little party. They were really excited; they sang songs for us, in French of course.

Romayne is in the green dress.

Also had a beautiful cocktail Xmas party here in the apartment. We had cocktails and cooked our dinner, lit the sparklers on the tree and candles, and opened presents between roommates. Nannette gave me a neat pair of ski poles and a bottle of whiskey. We were all dressed up and later some of the American fellows same over and we all went out. The "kids" that live in the apartment with me are really great! Of course, we had a Xmas party in the Villa before we left and a big Xmas dinner. We also gave a few skits for entertainment and I was in one of them.

We have a study group for all Americans in Fribourg. Every other week someone leads a discussion on some topic and I have to lead the next one Jan. 20. Will probably do it on advertising since it is the only book in English we have which would fit in the discussions.

Mrs. Ladwig wrote Nannette about you inviting them over to see my "movies". She seems to like you and had a good time while she and Mr. Ladwig were over. That's about all for now.....write soon.

Love, Ro

P.S. Mom got your neat pen. Very impressive!!

Still waiting to hear from Susie about Brownies and see her new school picture.

Romaine and Peter Troost

Chapter 5

Student Life at the Villa and Sarina

January 12, 1960

Villa des Fougeres Fribourg, Suisse
January 12, 1960

Dear Mom and Dad, everything is fine. I have been good, healthy, studying, and also having a good time. I have no idea what Nannette wrote her parents that should warrant such a letter as the one you wrote to me, Mom. I ask Nannette and she doesn't remember writing anything about an "apartment incident" that is serious. As far as the apartment is concerned it is true they threatened to evict all of us because at times we make a little too much noise. Sister Benvenuta has also been upset about the noise; however, the manager blames us for all the noise and lots of times the people in the apartment above us make more noise that we do, and have huge parties plus playing their radio loud all the time.

Perhaps Nannette wrote her parents about the man down the hall from us who has been arrested for giving abortions. He was a Jewish man from the States. Nannette and I knew him and he was always very nice to us. He never even gave us any reason to think he wasn't just a plain ordinary doctor. We also know his friends who are medical students here from the States. They have always been nice and one of them treats us like he is our father. Honestly Mother, those are the only two "apartment incidents" I can think of if you will please tell me directly what you are referring to I will be glad to explain it.

Ordered my watch from Luzern, haven't received it as yet and therefore don't know how much it will cost.

About my sailing home, Nannette received a letter from her mother stating that Sister George is working on our passage for Aug. 30

or Sept. 6. Prefer to sail home August 30, because I want to spend a couple of days in New York visiting my friends, then some time at home before returning to the University of Colorado. Don't know yet if we will be accepted at the Univ. of Oslo. Filled out the application, but have to write a 250 word theme why I want to go there before I can send it in....hope to do this this weekend. Promise to let you know as soon as possible whether I am accepted at the Univ. of Oslo for summer school or not. Don't know what to tell you about whether to cancel my present reservation or not now because I don't know about Oslo as yet.

Still waiting to hear about the car I wish to buy. If I am not accepted at Oslo, would like to visit a friend of mine in Spain. Met a girl in Vienna who is now living with her mother in Spain from the States. She came back to Fribourg to stay with me for a few days when we returned from Christmas vacation. She lives in Majorca and has invited Nannette and me to visit her any time.

Last Sunday my friend from Spain and I went to lunch at the apartment of a Swiss and Yugoslavian. They cooked lunch for us and then we all sat around and talked and drank Yugoslavian wine. Just good friends!

Sister Benvenuta will probably write you a letter about my spring plans for the Middle East and Italy. We were going to go with her to Italy and then leave the group. But now we think we can do Italy at half the price she is charging and might do it on our own. She wants $200 for the bus from Fribourg to Venice, Florence, and Rome including room and board. There is a train which students can take anywhere in Italy $22.50 for fifteen days. We can take this train, room and board, and guide fees for half of what Sister B. is charging.

There are six of us here in the apartment that plan not to go with the group. I am not sure if Nannette will go with us all the way because her aunt is coming over here to travel with her. Her aunt has to leave April 1 st for the States so Nannette will probably meet us at our friend's house in Iran,

Vida, from Iran, said her father is thinking about hiring a plane to take all of us around. Her father is head of the Iranian army. Sister Benvenuta said we will have to fly if we leave her group. However, this is too expensive and now we are working on a way to get around this rule of hers. She said she was going to write our folks about what we are planning to do for she thinks her trip is best. However, I don't know if we will ever get another chance like this to go to Vida's house in Tehran, Iran and don't think we should pass this chance up. Will need permission from home to go, but do not write Sister Benvenuta, please, until I give you the details and what she should know.

Have to run to class now at the University...Write Soon.

Love, Ro

P. S. Please drop the enclosed card in the nearest mailbox. It doesn't need any stamps.

Villa des Fougeres Fribourg, Suisse
January 22, 1960

Dear Mere and Pere,

First of all, mailing my application this afternoon with my theme on why I want to go to the University of Oslo and scholarship form. Please drop the enclosed letter to the Univ. of Colorado with one dollar and 4 cents. I don't have any American money to send. I still need the following things, which you will have to get for me and send to St. Olaf College in Northfield, Minnesota, as soon as possible please!

- Two letters of recommendation by persons not related to me by blood or marriage. Giving information regarding my character, intellectual ability and seriousness of purpose. One of these letters must come from a professor or principal. (Try Sister George perhaps)

- A doctor's statement certifying my present health conditions.

January 28, 1960

Working on Visas now for the Middle East. Please send my birth certificate <u>and</u> baptismal record as soon as possible. Will mail you our exact itinerary as soon as it is completed.

Dad, I was glad to receive your letter, info on Oslo, and Income Tax Form. Still haven't received my form from Macy's telling me how much I get back as yet. Dad, does your car insurance cover me? Can't wait to see the elves you gave Susie and hear their latest names....think that is a riot!!!

Mom, what is the latest on your campaign? Wrote Bucherer in Luzern and they will sell me the watch for about $31 with only a finger band. Did my last letter explain whatever was bothering you well enough...still waiting to hear from you.

January 30, 1960

Latest flash on the Middle East trip.... It is going to cost a bit more than expected but it is going to be much more fabulous!!! Vida's mother and father came today to visit her on their way home from London. They are wonderful people and don't seem to be able to be good enough to us. General Kia is going to rent an army airplane to show us around. They want us to go to the Caspian Sea for a few days. And, Mrs. Kia said of course we will have to have a great big party for you all when you come. At present we were planning to stay four days but they want us to stay more. Their house must be huge because we are all ten of us going to stay in the same room. April 4th is a big day in Tehran and they said we must come for it, because everyone goes out of town and General Kia takes all his friends to his Villa and they have a native ceremony. The whole event is supposed to be fabulous! He said because of the Middle Eastern situation at this time it would be better if we didn't go to Baghdad in Iraq. All the other countries are okay at this time, and if not in the future he will let us know. General Kia is some big big deal in the army because there in only one man on top of him and his position is honorary. Of course, their family went to the Shah's wedding and gave him some huge solid gold plaque with jewels all over it and Persian writing. I suppose by this time Nannette's aunt has told you about her connections in different cities. Personally I think this is probably going to be a chance in a lifetime experience and would love to go.

January 31, 1960

(Sorry about the interruption, but I had a date last night and had to go.)

Back to Tehran....General Kia said at his Villa we can go donkey, camel, or horseback riding. April 4th is the Moslem New year, I just found out.

Generally our trip is going to go as follows...Geneva, Rome, Cairo, Beirut, Damascus, Tehran, Istanbul, Ankara, Athens, Naples, Capri, and Venice and back to Geneva. Most of these stops there is someone to meet us and show us around. Also, General Kia said, since we can't go to Baghdad to go to the Holy Land, he didn't think it would be much more expensive and he would have someone meet us to show us around in Tel Aviv. The only thing is it is cheaper to do all this by plane than by bus, boat, and train. However, the price for the whole trip will run about $700. I realize this is quite a lot of money for 44 days. But, transportation will run us not more than $480. And, if we cut way down on pleasure spending we think we can live cheaply and get by with $220 for room and board. We won't really need any guides since most of the stops we have prominent people meeting us. If you feel this is too much money, I am willing to pay you some of it back when I get out of college and get a permanent job. I promise as soon as I start working I will pay back so much a week. Please write soon and let me know what you think of this trip. Also, talk to Mrs. Ladwig and Mrs. de la Croix our chaperon for the details. By the way, we also have another chaperon who is going all the way with us. She is one of the aunts of the other girls, who lives in Milwaukee, Wisconsin. Please check in the vault box and see if I have any bonds to be cashed. This is only $200 more than Sister Benvenuta's trip.

I am now a full-fledged Sarina fraternity member. Two Monday's ago they had the initiation....I had to shave my date (only cut him once on the chin). Then the president gave me my ribbons. We drank champagne together and kissed on each cheek (great European custom)! Then I had to drink champagne with the fellow in charge of the program and my date. Then everyone clapped and now I am an active member!!!!

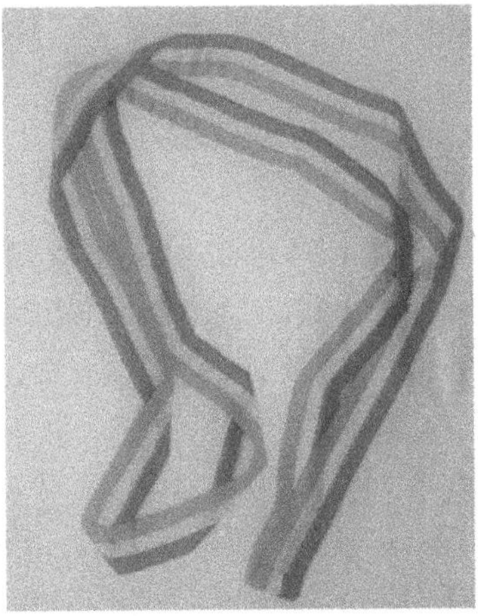

Sarina had its huge ball last Saturday night. The decorations were beautiful....they consisted of branches of roses hanging from the walls and ceiling. The orchestra was excellent and all the girls got corsages. I wore my green cocktail dress you bought me for Xmas last year and everybody loved it. The Swiss people really dressed for the occasion. There were also some professors there and older people who were once members of Sarina. At 12:30am everyone threw confetti and streamers which livened things up again. You would have thought it was New Year's Eve. Sister Benvenuta let me stay out until 3:00am, although the ball didn't end until five or six o'clock. Fabulous time!

Then the next day Sunday they had a tea dance for all. Fun, fun, fun!!!

Have to get ready for church now and want to get this in the mail on the way...so that's about all for now...hope to hear from you all soon. Tell Susie I promise to write her a letter soon, don't have time now.

Love, Romayne

Villa des Fougeres Fribourg, Suisse
Feb. 7, 1960

Dear Mom and Dad,

Was glad to receive both of your letters and the Valentine. By the way, how is the new maid working out? Mom, Thanks for sending the records I needed, we are working on all of our visas needed right now.

To keep things straight...I definitely want to come home on the Holland American Line on the 30th the Rotterdam. I don't want to come home on a Norwegian Line because I will have to stop in Munich and pick up the car for Dad. Besides the Norwegian Line is slower and I would have to leave here earlier to get home at the same time.

By the way, Dad check and see what address I should give for your car to pay the lowest taxes. I think if I can give a Colorado address the taxes are cheaper. Also, see if it would be possible for me to give Nannette's school address in Wisconsin, because Wisconsin doesn't have a state tax on each article. Also, let me know what to do about insurance.

Be sure to let me know when and where Bud, Dick, and Bob are going to be in Europe this summer. Perhaps somewhere along the way we can all meet. And also, I can write my friends and let them know that they are coming for it really helps to know someone in the different cities to show you around. Also, I can tell them what I thought about different places to go at night where there is a young crowd.

Enclosed is the schedule of our trip. Please sign this copy and send it directly to Sister Benvenuta, not to me, if it is okay for me to go ahead as planned. This is the completed schedule. The man at the American Express in Bern has drawn it up and is making all of our arrangements. It is going to cost exactly $486.20 for transportation by plane. Also, General Kia is going to have a man meet us in Tel Aviv to show us around.

Most of the current news is in the enclosed letter to Susie. Exams are the week of the 15th so you probably won't hear from me until they are over, unless something spectacular turns up. Have lots of work to do. Write soon...Happy Valentine's Day...miss you all.
Love, Ro

P. S. Actually, not all of us are going to stay in Athens that long, but plan to leave Sat. before Easter Sunday and be in Rome for Easter Sunday. Then we are going to stop in Florence and Venice on the way home. Also, plan to go down to Naples when we are in Rome for the first time. But, it is much simpler if we all just send the same thing to Sister Benvenuta.

P.S.S. The American Express man would like $200 to start processing our reservations. Or if you prefer send all of it, $486.20, as soon as possible.

February 8

Talked to my friend Susie this morning who lives in Riverside. She said her mother was going to call Mom. So I thought I had better warn you and tell you something about her.

Susie Herkes is the girl I palled around with most of the time in the fall and Christmas trip along with Nannette. When we were in

Cologne we went to see the family she lived with when she was over in Germany for high school one year. She lives in the Villa and not with me. But, we are still the best of friends. Met her parents for a minute when they were here before Xmas. She is also the other American member of my fraternity.

Villa des Fourgeres Fribourg, Suisse
February 25, 1960

Dear Mom and Dad,

Well, my exams are over for the most part now. I had six exams last week, and only have two more next week. I have quite a few because most of my courses are only one or two hours per week. But, in my French Literature of the 17th and 18th Century that is three hours long, I got an A-. I am extremely pleased because there was only one other A which was also a minus. Also, when the teacher gave back the papers in class he went over my paper for about five minutes and told the class I was the only one who really wrote a dissertation like he wanted. This is really quite a victory for me because at the beginning of the year, I explained to him what difficulty I was having understanding him and he told me "to drop the course." He told the whole class how astonished he was that I was the one with the best mark! Besides, on the major question I chose to write on, I didn't even have the time to read in the English books you sent me.

Everything I wrote came out of my class notes. Haven't gotten back any of my other exams as yet.

Before I forget, PLEASE send me immediately air mail a bottle of pills. The prescription number is 157431 and the doctor's name is Dr. Fox. The date of the bottle is 2/4/56. It is impossible for me to get these pills here. I had the prescription filled before I left but I only have one pill left. If you don't have time to send them call Heintz and have them send them to me or else have Nannette's aunt bring them to me. I will definitely need them before I leave for the Middle East!!!

I really like it here because I have lots of friends and really feel like

I belong here.

Actually this town even though it is small, is “tons of fun” if one goes out looking for the fun and to meet the people who live here. Last week I went for tea at one of the Swiss girls homes down in the Bas-Ville. It was really interesting in one room they even had one of those old title furnaces you usually see in the corner of rooms in old castles. The furniture was old but nice. And, the view from the window was beautiful of the mountains and the river running down through the old part of town.

This coming Friday night my fraternity puts on their play “Le Maitre de Santiago”. Susie and I are going to help by distributing programs before the play begins. We have already had to look for advertisements for their program along with the other girl members. I got one from my “camera man” and one from the Corso (local tearoom-bar we all go to). I read the play in French last night and this morning so I will be able to understand it and discuss it with people.

Then Sat, Sun, Mon, and Tue nights Fribourg has its grand carnival. It is really supposed to be gay. According to one of my Swiss friends everyone in the town waits for it from the chambermaid to the ladies in high society. Then at the balls everyone wears masks and “goes Wild”.

Plans for the Middle East are shaping up beautifully. Nannette’s aunt has a lot of contacts for us. Then Vida’s folks have decided to get musicians for us. I understand you already got addresses of the places we will visit. I suppose the best idea would be to write me in care of the American Express in the different cities and for a return address put my Villa des Fougeres address. Have some extra visa pictures and am sending one to show you my new hairstyle.

Received a letter yesterday from a friend of the girl I know in San Francisco inviting me down to Monte Carlo some time. Am thinking of going down for Pentecost because we have a four-day vacation and it is over my birthday weekend. Besides I understand you have to be 21 to go into the Casinos and I will be just 21! Fun, fun, fun!

Mom, saw the beautiful write up the Glen Ellyn News gave you. It was a good picture of you too. However, that is our town newspaper. Be careful because you know all the strength Hoffman has. Perhaps if you just get your name before the public this time, and if you don't win, at least next time you run more people will know who you are and the Democratic Party will be stronger and you will have more credit to your name. Please let me know how things progress.

Say "hello" to Susie and the boys for me. That's about all for now...

Love, Ro

P.S. Don't forget the pills. Very important.

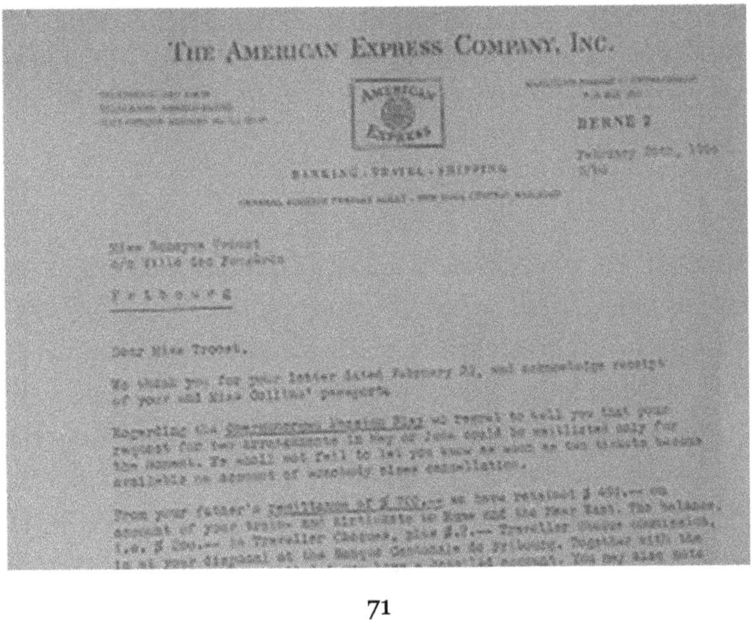
The American Express Company, Inc.

Banking . Travel . Shipping

Dear Miss Trost,

[illegible]

(Written on the reverse side of the letter from The American Express Company, February 26, 1960)

Dear Mom and Dad,

The other side pretty well explains things at the present time. The "Passion Play" referred to only comes once in ten years. It is supposed to be fantastic but now all of the tickets are sold and will have to wait for a cancellation.

My camera is now fixed perfectly according to my "camera man". He only charged me about 45 cents for postage to and from Zurich.

Friday morning

Dad was glad to receive your letter today. The man at the American Express already took money out for Travelers Checks so I took them. Don't pay your bank for them. He sent them here and I had to pay a slight charge to the bank here for handling them. I definitely can cash personal checks without any trouble or fee.

Having trouble getting an order for my car. Called Munich about a week ago and the man said I should get the order in the mail the next day, but haven't received it yet.

Evening

Well, bought my car today here in Fribourg. It cost the same price as in Munich and I can get delivery May 1st or just after I return!! I don't have to pay Swiss customs because I am exporting it. Really making progress in French because we did the whole transaction without a word of English! However, my French accent and construction still aren't very good because I live with Americans and talk English most of the time. Would love to stay another year and really perfect it. Back to the car, it will cost about $1,220 depending on the exchange at the time I have my money exchanged. Dads when you take my money out, send it directly to me so I can hold it until I can get a good exchange. The man said insurance, license, license plates etc. would cost about $100. They are going to teach me to drive it! Didn't order a radio, would be about $50 completely installed. What do you think? Now, it has a sunroof and U.S. specifications. It is a pretty shade of green. Has a guarantee for 10,000 kilometers about 6,000 miles. Also, can buy both cars in my name because I am buying them in different countries.

Besides, if anything goes wrong, I won't have to go to Munich.

If I bought your Mercedes here could get delivery in about two months. But, couldn't bring both cars from Swiss. Perhaps I could get it in France for you and not pay French customs if you prefer. Or one of the boys could bring it back, and I could order it here. Still can do it as we planned. Won't work, you have to be a resident of the country for three months. Could buy it in Nannette's name here.

Carnival here was fun! But, our hours were terrible. Carnival was Mon., Tue., and Wed. We could only go out one night until 12:30am. My Spanish friend has left for Madrid, so I met a new fellow. He's Swiss real nice about 6'8"!! Everyone was dressed from head to foot in costumes. Loads of balls all "packed" with people. Really fun. But no parades.

Sunday, Patty who lives with me, and I are going to hitchhike to Basel for the Carnival there. It starts 1:00am with a huge parade. We are taking off school Monday and returning Tuesday morning before class. We never have any "cuts" here but can take off one day about every four months. This is the biggest celebration in Suisse. People come from all over to see it! It is even in Patty's guidebook for Suisse!!! There are supposed to be lots of parades, balls (open to the public) and grotesque costumes!!

Haven't received the rest of my grades except a B in Theology. Leaving here Friday the 11th. Hope to hear from you along the way. Love, Ro.

Villa des Fougeres Fribourg, Suisse
February 26, 1960 Friday

Dear Dad,

You are wonderful to send me all the money for my trip! However, when you send money please always send it directly to me. For, here in Fribourg at the train station we get the best exchange for American dollars. It is even better than in Bern. I still have about $500 worth of Travelers Checks so I am going to leave the remainder of the money you sent in the bank. The man at American Express sent the remainder of the money to a bank here in Fribourg. So do not pay for Travelers Checks at your bank.

However, if you have already paid for them let me know and I will go down and pick them up. Also, by sending money directly to me you don't have to pay a bank transfer charge.

Regarding the cars, I wrote the man in Munich at the Volkswagen place two letters and never received a reply. So yesterday I called him and he said he never got my letters, but would send me another order immediately. I explained to him about putting the in Nannette's name, which is fine with her. However, Dad, now I can't get the car until the 10th of July and I have to be in Oslo before then. I explained this to the man and he said he would do the best he could but couldn't promise anything. Therefore, if it comes in later I will have to pick it up after summer school. This is rather inconvenient because Nannette and I can't get reservations on the Holland American Line for August 30 and will have to take the Norwegian Line from Oslo. This way when school is out I will have to go to Munich and back to Oslo before going home. I am working on reservations though American Express for the Rotterdam, but I don't think they will come through fast enough. I have to let the

Norwegian Line know by the 29th of February.

By the way, please thank Mr. McHugh for writing a recommendation for me. It was very nice the things he said and I appreciate it. Will let you know immediately when I hear from St. Olaf's about being accepted.

Understand your position about mother running for political office. Tried to say something in the letter I wrote to the house today. But, you know Mom when she goes out for something she goes all the way. Perhaps you can explain to her if she loses financially it will be difficult for her to run again. Whereas, this time if she gets her name on the ballot, but doesn't go all out and spend a fantastic sum of money, at least more people will hear of her. By the next election perhaps she will have a better chance because the Democratic Party will be built up more and she will have more credit to her name. Right now I think it best if she would worry about getting her degree, and then plunge "whole hog" into politics. If there is anything I can say to her you think will help please let me know.

By the way, how is the battle against the cemeteries working out? Do you still have the same secretary as before? Also, how is your new bookkeeper working out? If we still have the maid you told my about at home and she is not working out well, check the Glen Ellyn News. They always seem to have people who want that type of work.

I don't know for sure if I will make it to Sorrento during Easter vacation. If I do, do you still want the cigarette boxes? You told me you wanted a dozen that played music. Can I still declare them as part of my $500 duty free if I bring back a car? Otherwise, I will ship them directly to you.

Last roll of movie film I took only the first half and the last half turned out. The middle is absolutely black. I took it to my camera shop a couple of weeks ago. The man said he would send it to Zurich for a "check-up". Have to go in Monday and get it. Will let you know how it works out.

I am leaving here March 11th for vacation. Hope to hear from you before this.

Love, Ro

P.S. Haven't received a statement from Macy's California yet about my income tax. What should I do?

Chapter 6

Spring Break Trip to the Middle East

March 23, 1960

The Nile Hilton (stationary) Cairo, Egypt
March 23, 1960

Dear Mom and Dad, the things that have been happening are so fantastic, I expect to wake up and find myself dreaming any minute. Sorry I haven't had a chance to write sooner but I haven't even had a chance to sleep much.

To start with we "hit" Rome! We met the most wonderful group of Italian fellows. They are all students in Rome, well educated, fun, interesting and some of the most wonderful fellows you could ever meet. They took us sightseeing and told us the history behind everything. Two of them had an apartment on the top floor of an old building near the Fountain of Trevi. Second night in Rome we spent at their apartment eating spaghetti, dancing, listening to Italian music and being serenaded!! One of the fellas was the son of a count and had a huge chateau with 113 rooms in Assisi. We were all invited there. Off we went for two days, aunt included. One of the fellows was the cook. When we were hungry, he would go up to the chicken coop, catch the chickens, kill them, clean them, and cook us all dinner. Each meal we would also have spaghetti. Giorgio was the name of our excellent cook. Assisi is an historic town built in the eighth century. There is nothing modern about it. You feel as if you are living in the Middle Ages!

The fellows were all real gentlemen and didn't expect anything for all they gave us. They came to see us off at the plane. The one I was with gave me his little frog that was his good luck piece. We were always in a group with these fellows. They were the happiest, good-hearted, terrific fellows you could ever want to meet. Also, got an audience with the Pope.

Antonello

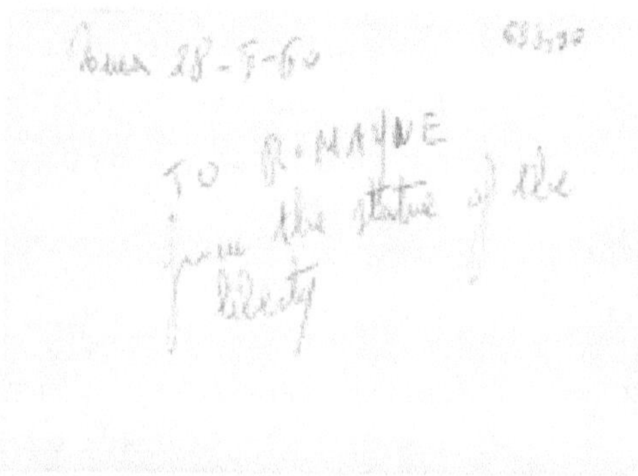

Roma 28-5-60

TO ROMAYNE
from the statue of the
liberty

We hated to leave Rome, but Beirut proved to be equally as wonderful. On the plane, I met Mr. James Weldon and his wife who work for the United Nations in the refuge plan for the Jews from Palestine. This program clothes, feeds, and educates these people. He said the older people accept their present condition, but it is hard on the younger people for all they have is an Israel passport and can't go anyplace. Nazir a Beirutian from our class in Fribourg and all his relatives met us at the airport. Also, we were met by friends of Nannette's aunt. Went out with the first group of fellows for a drink. Then at 10:00pm went out with Nannette's aunt's friends to two of the best nightclubs in Beirut!!

Beirut itself looks like a paradise. The country is hilly situated between the mountains and the Mediterranean Sea. The town in parts is very American because its buildings are modern. You find American music, cars, and food. You can get "Chicken-in-the-Basket", hot dogs, American breakfasts and any other American food. At night Beirut is beautiful. You can see all the lights of the little villages in the mountains. The first day we went swimming in the Mediterranean Sea. Ate lunch at "Hagi Baba" which is very oriental. Then we went up in the mountains and got a fabulous view of the city. At night we went to one of the best Lebanese restaurants for Lebanese food. To start they served 100 dishes of appetizers, then "Schkebob" sp?, and a dessert with orange flowers that smelled like perfume. During the rest of the week we visited mosques (which are Moslems churches. One has to put on cloth shoes over regular shoes to go through because when the Moslems pray they touch their heads to the floor. The market places are fascinating. They are noisy, dirty, pushing, arguing about price, and every imaginable article for sale. Bought a neat looking Moslem outfit for Dad. Wanted to send it to you for your birthday but there was a mix up on sending and it is being sent to one of the girls with us in New York, It is really "whippy" looking. Dad, I thought you could probably wear it when you have cocktail parties. Also, bought a huge brass tray for your anniversary, which is also being sent to New York. Will pick them up on the way home. Mom, for your birthday in Damascus I ought a huge dining room table cloth with 12 napkins. It is the same color as the dining room drapes and has beautiful gold embroidery all over it. I have been taking tons of pictures so you can have a fantastic party when I come home. In Beirut we also saw a huge orchard with lemons the size of grapefruits. Just outside of Beirut at Sidon they have an old fortress built by the Phoenicians. At Balbek, we saw Roman Ruins of huge temples built to their gods such as Venus and Bacchus.

They have tons of nightclubs, which we visited. Went over to Mr. Weldon's apartment, United Nations man I met on the plane. He and his wife are two of the most wonderful intelligent, friendly people that can be found anywhere. We discussed everything including my major. I think now I am going to major in economics. I really enjoyed the one course I took in it. It should give me a solid background in whatever I finally decide to do once I get out of school or go on with further studies.

The people we knew and met in Beirut and their families were wonderful to us. Cousins, uncles, brothers, and friends would take us all sightseeing for we never split up. One friend that became attached to us was Moustapha Inja. His grandfather used to be the tyrant of this area and head of it all before the change in government. We even visited his grandfather's palace with him.

We all took taxis to Damascus and he came with us. Damascus is a typical Arab city. It is small and has a weird strangle air to it. Visited the museum, open and closed air markets, place where Saint Paul was lowered down from the wall to leave the city, one of the biggest mosques. At night we went out with the same Syrian college students that were friends of Nannette's aunt.

Back to Beirut the next evening. Before we left Nazir, friend from Fribourg, had us all over for a huge Lebanese lunch.

Cairo was unbelievable! I have never in my life met so many nice, wonderful, kind, hospitable people. People who only know us as strangers and yet treat us like queens. First of all the Hilton gave us special rates of $2.25 a night. First night, I had one of the most beautiful hotel rooms I have ever seen facing the Nile River!! However, since rates came way down, we were soon changed to a smaller room for four in the back. We were met by friends and taken to one of the most fashionable nightclubs for dinner, floor show, and dancing. Next day explored the pyramids while riding camels!! Met one of the Hilton's tour guides who took us all around free since we were "poor students". The strange thing about Egypt is that you have the modern alongside the ancient. In the same street you can see people riding donkeys and new American cars! You can see people in Western clothing and at the same time many people, men and women, wearing robes that resemble "pajamas". And, many women are all in black with veils covering their faces. Visited the "King Tut" museum. It was fascinating to see all the "junk" they throw into one tomb including petrified food, and animals etc. Found a guide who again took us around the museum free because we were students. Also visited the bazaars and mosques.

Took two side trips while in Cairo, one to Alexandria and the other to the Suez Canal at Ismailea. While in Alexandria we saw King Farouk's palaces. They are gorgeous, huge, enormous things. Had an enormous lunch with friends there. Mom and Dad, at the time we hit Cairo the Moslems were having Ramadan, which is the month when they don't eat, drink, or smoke from daylight to sunset. Yet these people would prepare feasts for us. And, you could never eat enough. They were always giving you more to eat and drink. The man we had lunch with took us through his factory where they make Egyptian cotton. By the way, took a private bus to and from Alexandria and had to pass through the desert. Our guide pointed out houses and trees on one side of the road that were really mirages for they were actually eight to ten miles on the other side of the road. But, when the clouds are low all this reflects across.

In the Hilton, we met Negmedine Shahin the man in charge of the Health Department for the Suez Canal. He invited us up for the day. He picked us up early in the morning. While he worked in the morning, we swam, sailed, and watched the huge ships pass through the Canal.

We went swimming in one of the lakes of the Canal. In the afternoon, he took us out for lunch and for a drive along the canal. Luckily we got to take the road along the canal for employees only.

The night we left this man and his friend took us out for a farewell dinner. Before dinner we went to his friend's house for drinks. Our host lived in a mansion on the Nile. Before he even asked us to stay for dinner he had places set for us!! Met a wonderful woman there, Tania Shahin, who has invited me to stay with her for <u>at least</u> a month. Her husband and her mother and sons would be there so I would be well chaperoned. These people have really shown me wonderful hospitality and the amazing thing is they don't want anything for it!!

Now we are in Jerusalem, Jordan. I am very disappointed because everything is covered with churches. All you can see is a piece of some original rock inside a church. We have gone to Bethlehem, Jericho, and the Dead Sea, besides all over Jerusalem. Went swimming in the Dead Sea, which was a lot like Salt Lake in Utah. Dad, I bought you a beautiful crucifix all hand carved out of olive wood in Bethlehem. Will bring it home with me.

Sorry I haven't had more time to write. The political situation is calm. Mom, I am insulted because you think I look like a Jew. Please don't worry about me. I promise to stay with the group at all times. Mom, I received your letter in Cairo and was very happy you took time out to write me. Haven't received any other mail. I am healthy, happy and have never had such a fantastic vacation! People keep us going all day and all night so if you don't hear from me for a while please don't worry. Mr. Weldon of the UN assured me I was safe here.

Love, Ro

P.S. Also had our pictures taken in Cairo for the local paper!!

ISTANBUL HILTON
April 13, 1960

(Stationery) Istanbul, Turkey Cable: Hiltels Istanbul Telephone: 483200

Dear Mom and Dad,

This is the third letter —hope you have received the other two. Mom was glad to receive your second letter at Vida's – dying to hear how the election turned out!! Please let me know immediately.

Have not as yet heard from the University of Colorado. Did you send them the letter I wrote requesting my grades sent to Oslo and a re-entrance blank? Wrote for a room in my sorority house before I left Fribourg.

Dad, also wrote my boss for an income tax statement. Received a letter from her at Vida's and she has sent one to me. Is it too late to file a regular return?

I have been having a horrible time getting boat reservations in August. Vida's brother got us the only ones possible. I have tourist class reservations on the Constitution of American Export Lines leaving August 23rd from Cannes in southern France and arriving New York August 31.

Mom, I have no idea of who Bob Cummiskey is. Write me and let me know what he looks like or where he goes to school. And, I will write him a thank you note for you.

Tell Frank he better be nice to me when I get home because I bought him stamps from Syria, Israel, and Iran so far. Will try to buy Susie a doll—have been trying to think of something to buy her.

Before I continue with the events of my trip since the last letter—have decided what I would like for my birthday—a gold ring made up with our family crest on it. Many Europeans have them and they really look sharp! My ring size is about 5 ½ or 6. What do you think of the idea?

Back to Teheran Wednesday April 6th. Started the morning off by going to Iran's largest textile factory. Vida's first cousin is the manager of it. The United States built it under the Point Four Program. The Iranian government paid the Americans to build it and run it for seven years to teach their people how to operate such a mill. It produces cheap cotton for the poor. Then off to a middle class restaurant (all of us guests of one of the Kia's friends). We ate one of the most popular Iranian dishes called a Chello Kebab which consisted of mixing rice, raw egg, onions and lamb together. Actually it tastes very good. Afternoon we spent in the markets and university. The university has a very pretty campus and about thirty men stood staring at all of us. At night we stayed at Vida's.

Persian society is different from ours. First of all, the Kias are one of the top and richest families in Iran. Young people do not go out on dates with anyone like we do in the States. If they go out, the family must approve the boy. And they must be chaperoned at all times. While Vida was at school between Christmas and spring, her folks received six proposals for her and only two of them were worthy enough. Girls that go out with men on dates, even if they don't do anything wrong are very much looked down upon. Out of the house, Vida always has to act dignified because all her actions reflect on her father's position.

Thursday, April 7th General Kia got us an army plane to see the South of Iran. ("Us" includes seven girls I am traveling with, Betty's aunt "who is a doll", Vida and two girls from "the apartment" who are staying with Vida for the whole vacation, two girls from River Forest going to school in Paris, and a boyfriend of one of the girls.) So Colonel Kia, cousin and chaperon, fourteen girls and one fellow, all spent the next few days gratis of General Kia including room and board. Met at Isphahan by various army officers including a general. "Whisked off" to Officers Club where we ate and spent the night. All treated like queens!! Five little men were always outside our door to open and shut it and "jump" to our every need. Took a tour of the city in private cars with two colonels, one major and our pilot along for escorts. For the most part, we saw beautiful old mosques with blue tile walls and huge minarets (took pictures).

Divided up for shopping with escort for chaperon and do the bargaining. The service we received was unbelievable—every time we would stop someplace our driver would run around the car fast as possible to open our doors.

Next morning after waiting for one half hour at the airport for water pipes—that we all decided at the last minute—we must have and bidding farewell to the general and his wife, we flew to Shiraz. The pilot and I became good friends so he let me fly the plane for about 15 minutes before we landed—even got to circle the city!! There is nothing to flying. Mom, it is just like driving a car without traffic except there are two additional controls on the wheel, pull forward for climbing and pushing for a dive.

Continue trip from Athens—have got to leave for plane now.

Love, Romayne

Villa des Fougeres Fribourg, Suisse
April 27, 1960

Dear Mom and Dad,

It is really good to be back in Switzerland. At the moment I feel completely traveled out. My vacation to the Middle East was really fantastic and something I will never forget. But, on the other hand it is hard to be traveling and going every minute for six weeks.

Mom, it was real good to receive your letter. I'm sorry to hear about the election. But, the way you seem to be taking the results after all the work you must have done is really something to be admired. About school, I definitely think you should finish now. If the work seems to be too much, throw out your text books – buy some College Outline Series for most of your courses, read the summaries in your books for each chapter, take good notes, and for your exams study only that and I am sure you will at least come out with C's. Concentrate the rest of your time on any papers you have to do. It seems a shame to let it go now so close to the end, even if you get D's you will still graduate. I already wrote to the University of Colorado on the letter I sent home for you to mail concerning having my grades sent to Oslo. If you haven't written them yet, forget it because another girl from the University of Colorado here has written for blanks for herself and me yesterday.

Mom, I am excited about your meeting me in New York!! It would really be fun if you could make it. Will let you know final details about the reservations as soon as Vida comes back here to Fribourg. If you are planning to meet me in New York, remember I will have my car. If you want we can drive back to Glen Ellyn together so don't make train reservations. Nannette is definitely going to fly back to the States, but Vida, Betty, and three American fellows I know are sailing on the same ship.

Have not bought my watch yet, but for Ascension Thursday we have a free day and Sister Benvenuta is taking us all to Luzern by bus so I will get it at that time. It will cost about $31.00. Don't worry about my red spring coat, for remember you bought me a brown spring coat before I left for Europe. I have worn it on the fall trip and the past spring trip. It has worked out wonderfully!

I am glad to hear Bob and Bud are going to Europe this summer. I plan to write Bud a letter as soon as I finish this one. Maybe I can meet them someplace after summer school until I leave. At any rate the people I know over here I am sure will be glad to show them around. I already told my friends in Italy they are coming and they will be glad to help them out. I am sorry Dick isn't coming with them.

I haven't really had much more trouble with my ankle except of this last trip. Both of my ankles swelled up after a lot of walking or wearing high heels for a long period of time.

I received a letter from American Express this morning saying he got me tickets to the Oberammergau Passion Play held in Germany!!! This play only takes place once in every ten years. Tickets are extremely hard to get. It is supposed to be something one can't afford to miss. I have had my request in for a long time. I am very lucky to get tickets. Susie Herkes from Riverside is going with me. It will cost $19 per person including two nights' accommodation at a private home, all meals, and first class admission tickets to the play. You have to buy your room and board with the tickets. Sister Benvenuta has given us permission to go for the 29th of May!

Latest flash about Oslo—Sister Benvenuta has agreed to let us out of school early so we can get up to Norway for the first day of school there. We will leave here on July 1st and school starts there July 4th. Will try to get my health certificate tomorrow to send to them. Received my acceptance from Oslo. They didn't say anything about my scholarship I applied for, but they did mention that my mother world pay the fees. Mom, you must of made them think I didn't have any need for a scholarship.

Vida's back...this is definitely what I am going to do about reservations coming back to the States. I am leaving August 23 from Cannes, France along the Rivera. I will arrive in New York on August 31st in the afternoon. After summer school is out, I want to go back to the continent.

I definitely don't want to sail from Norway. It is going to cost $280 plus tax on the Constitution tourist class. Sister Benvenuta said she would write Sister George about getting my money back from the Holland American Line.

Can buy the ring I want over here. It will cost about $35.just for the ring without engraving.

That is in 18-karat gold. Then the engraving will run about $15. Maybe you could buy it cheaper in the States. Anyway, if you decide it is okay for me to buy it here please send me the family crest. This is quite a bit of money for a ring, but someday it probably will be a family heirloom.

Well back to my trip...the last time I wrote I think we were in Shiraz. Besides sightseeing we had dinner with the governor general. It was the craziest thing; we all stood up and ate! He had a buffet set up and instead of taking your dishes in the other room, everyone stood up and ate.

We were two days late getting out of Shiraz because the weather was too bad for the plane to take off. Finally we ended up going back to Isphahan by bus. It was a miserable ride for 12 hours over washboard roads. It rained, snowed, and was extremely muddy. Finally we stopped in the middle of nowhere for tea! Then about dinnertime we stopped again to eat. The colonel didn't know about the sanitation in the place so we all ate fried eggs on bread that looked like pancakes but was much larger. They didn't give us any silverware. The trick was to use the bread as a plate. Well, the first bite I took the egg went out the other end and landed on the table!!! Grace. Finally arrived about 2 am. Couldn't stay at the officers club again because they were expecting King Leopold of Belgium. Luckily the weather was nice the next day and our plane joined us once again. We flew up to Teheran. Vida's brother, who is married to a Swedish girl, gave us a big party. He is really a nice fellow, funny as they come. We had loads of food, drinks, and fun!!!

Finally got a plane out the next morning. Mrs. Kia, Vida, some general, and our colonel came to see us off. Flew KLM to Istanbul, think it is the best airline I have ever flown. Arrived in Istanbul without any place to stay so we went to the Istanbul Hilton. Told them we were poor students without any place to stay. After a long discussion we finally got two rooms with four in a room for $4.50 per night. Met a fellow there from Boston who had a single and was paying $14.50 per night so we did okay. Istanbul was cold the two days we were there which spoiled things in a way. The city itself is full of mosques with high towers that give the skyline a unique look. The Bosphorous, which is part of the sea that comes through the city, has many wharfs with old boats that make the entire city look very picturesque. Took a tour of the main mosques, underground cistern, markets, the white palace, and then to the home of our guide. His name was Camel Koran.

Flew to Greece and was met by Mr. Flick a friend of Betty's aunt. He was Dutch and took care of us while we were in Athens. Day we arrived we went over to his house for snacks. Then we took a tour of Athens. Athens is rather modern itself. However, in the midst of the city stands a hill with the Acropolis on it. At night Mr. Flick escorted us to an old Greek Taverna, which consists of a kind of beat place with pictures drawn on the walls. We ate the traditional Greek food that consisted of squid, which is octopus and tastes a little like lobster, caviar, grape leaves with chopped meat and rice inside, kabob, wine, and fruit. The next day we spend driving along the coast to the most southern point in Greece. The drive was really beautiful because there weren't any hotels, signs, and homes to spoil it. There is an old temple erected to Poseidon perched on the top of a hill overlooking the Aegean Sea. This was Good Friday. As we rode back through the countryside, you could see the churches jammed, people bringing flowers like a wake, and bells ringing. At night we hitchhiked into Athens to see the Good Friday Procession. It was really impressive. The entire city turned out. When the procession passed all the lights were turned out. There were boy scouts, ministers and officials, priests, bishops, and four men carrying what was to resemble the tomb of Christ, plus and military forces.

Patty and I ran into our friend we met in Istanbul in the airport. Stopped to have a drink with him. And, since we were the last two to get on the plane, we got to ride fist class! All the tourist seats were taken by this time. Wonderful flight, we had sherry before dinner, hot dinner with champagne, cognac, and cigarettes all free. It was sunny as we flew into Italy. Our Italian friends were waiting for us. They had a huge spaghetti dinner ready for us in their apartment. The apartment was all cleaned up with flowers. We had a big party with ice cream cake, Italian music and all our friends! It rained all day Easter Sunday. It was too miserable to try to fight the crowds at Saint Peter's so we just went to Saint Mary Major's Basilica for mass. It was a beautiful high mass with bishop and all. In the church we heard the papal benediction. Too miserable weather to go sightseeing so we spent the rest of the day with our Italian friends. Monday it rained again. But we went out to walk around the Coliseum, the Forum, and little church where lots of Hollywood movie stars get married, St Peter in Chains Church with the magnificent statue of Moses by Michelangelo. Tuesday, my Italian friend, Antonello, and I walked out to the catacombs. The sun shone finally and it was a beautiful walk. Thought the catacombs were interesting. We took an English guide and I had to translate for him in French. Had lunch at a little Italian restaurant on the way back with real good Italian food. However, on the way back it started to rain again. The rest of the group left for Florence on the afternoon train and I went on the night train. Didn't see them again until the train pulled out of Milan. But, it was really restful to be alone after traveling with a group for so long. Loved Florence, took an American Express tour that was excellent. The guide was an Italian. He knew all about the art and the artists. He could really give you a feeling for the painting. Hope to take some courses in art sometime when I get back to the States. Saw the rest of Florence on my own with a guidebook. Followed a few guides around some of the art museums that were excellent. Met a girl who is teaching school in Germany and went with her most of the time.

Being over here so long and seeing so much art, I am really developing an appreciation for it.

Especially after the excellent guide I had in Florence. I was really impressed by the statue of David by Michelangelo.

Went up to Venice on the night train. Horrible horrible ride stood all night because the trains were so crowed. All the soldiers were on vacation. I couldn't even get across from the seats to stand. Had to stand out by the "john" and every few minutes someone would push his way to the "john". However, one of the soldiers gave me his pack to sit on after a while so I survived.

Found a "grubby" hotel close to the station. I slept till noon and then proceeded to see the town. I love Venice with all its picturesque little streets none of them straight, canals, cafes and shops! Saw how Venetian glass was made and a beautiful masterpiece by Bellini and Titian. Next day my friend from Florence came to join me, really a cute gal. Went for a gondola ride through all the canals with a Norwegian I met in the hotel. Caught the 1:00 am train for Fribourg. Another horrible ride on a stuffed train. As the train came into picturesque Switzerland, it really felt good to be back again to a nice green country with mountains, lakes, and chateaus dotting the countryside!!!!

All in all it was a wonderful vacation, which I shall never forget. I took about 8 and one half rolls of film that I will send home as soon as I have the four I bought here in Switzerland with developing processed. Enclosed is a snapshot an Egyptian took and sent to me. I have made lots of new friends. If all the people I have invited to see me come at some time, we are sure to be running an international house. The people I invited have all been wonderful to me. I am sure the whole family will profit by talking to them.

Now, for a few words in regard to our chaperons. My opinion and the opinion of the other girls toward Mrs. De la Croix is that she is a snob, namedropper, and a complete phony. I would be interested in your opinion since you have also met her. Betty's aunt turned out to be a complete "doll". She is a load of fun, young in spirit and an interesting woman.

My Volkswagen has arrived. It will cost $1,250 with delivery charges.

Also, I will need about $100 for license, insurance, registration fees, and other necessities. Before you take all the money out of my bank account deposit a few dollars so they will figure up the interest I have coming to me. Then the next day take it all out. Just be sure leave at least a dollar so I will still have an account. Would appreciate your sending the money by check made out to me as soon as possible for the people want me to pick up the car.

Hope to hear from you all soon...
Love, Romayne

Chapter 7

Back to Student Life at the Villa

April 28, 1960

Heureux Anniversaire translates in English to Happy Birthday.

Message on Birthday Card:
April 28, 1960

Dear Dad,

Now that all the confusion is over at home, I hope you can relax and have a very Happy Birthday.

I requested a mass to be said for you at the beautiful basilica of Sacred Coeur (Sacred Heart) in Paris for your birthday. Sorry your present got mixed up and ended up in New York. Will bring it home in August.

Sincerely wish a very relaxing birthday to the most wonderful father in the world. With love—

Your daughter, Romayne

Villa des Fourgeres Fribourg, Suisse
May 10, 1960

Dear Mom and Dad,

First of all Dad I can't possibly send any money to Oslo because you have sent me all my money in Travelers Checks. It would be very impractical and a waste of money to cash them all in and send a money order. According to a letter I received lately, I guess I wasn't even considered for a scholarship because my grade transcript and health certificate weren't in on time. Therefore, the cost is going to be $275 including registration and student fee, six weeks tuition, six weeks board and room, and excursion fee. I suggest you send this money in right away. However, if it is too late, I can always make other summer plans – perhaps I will spend some time with the lady in Egypt who invited me stay with her this summer for at least one month and some time with my girlfriend who lives in Spain.

Second, my Volkswagen is ready. I am going to have to pick it up as soon as possible because have had it ever since I got back from vacation. PLEASE take my money out of the bank and send it as soon as possible. It is getting embarrassing.

Went hitchhiking this past weekend with Nannette, Patty, and Melon. We got one ride directly from Bern to Zurich with an inventor. His latest invention on the market is the crazy STOP*NOW device. Mom, definitely think you should buy one if you see them on the market. It is a device to check your speed. You just set it for the speed limit and every time you reach this mark a bell goes off. After about 3 more miles, the bell is automatically turned off. This way it wouldn't always be my fault for talking when you get a ticket!! We stayed in the old part of Zurich. Really had a "ball" because there were thousands of gay spots to hit! Next morning we all went rummaging around the town. Went to the Swiss National Museum that I feel is the best in Switzerland to see its culture, history and art. About 4:00 we decided to spend Saturday night in some town around Lucerne. But, a very nice man picked us up who was going to Andromatt a very picturesque little mountain town in the south of Switzerland, so we decided to go there. We stayed in a rather primitive hotel. There was no heat, huge feather puffs on the beds, and the washbasins consisted of huge porcelain pitchers of water and porcelain bowls!

About 10 pm a band marched down the street playing music because it was somebody's wedding reception! Sunday morning after mass, we climbed half way up a mountain and sat down to admire the little town. Everything was peaceful and quiet and occasionally the church bells would ring. It was really a beautiful sight to see this little town with its church spires reaching towards heaven completely surrounded by the mountains, which not only the tops were covered with snow. Where we were sitting there were patches of snow and alongside them were crocus in bloom. In descending down into the little town, we saw a man practicing on his Alpine horn with small children standing around watching him. There were men and small boys with their dogcarts carrying huge cans of milk. And, the women were dressed in their native costumes because it was Mother's Day! Leaving about 11:30 am, we drove down through the mountains with the same man who gave us a ride there. The mountains were really beautiful because being spring the snow was melting, and there were waterfalls all over! The man let us off at some little town across the lake from Luzern. The Lake of Luzern was magnificent with everything in bloom all around it! After various rides and finally splitting into twos at Luzern, we finally made it back to Fribourg before dark.

The weather has been beautiful lately. It has finally warmed up here. By the way, I will send the pictures this week. I had four rolls developed and had to pay for two because I got the boxes mixed up. I am sending home ten rolls of film: 5 are already developed. The other five rolls three have the developing already paid and it should be marked on the firm itself according to the cameraman here even if it is not marked on the boxes. Please let me know how it comes out.

Please, Dad, have Bud or Bob bring me some movie film from the States. It may take up some room in their suitcase, but they will want extra room to take things back with them from Europe anyway. Bob wrote and said they were coming the 25th of June and going right to Germany. So I should see them when I drive up to Oslo through Germany of if I don't go to Oslo in Switzerland. They can always leave the film at an American Express somewhere in Germany.

Hope to hear from you soon regarding Oslo and my car.

Love, Ro

HOTEL DE PARIS MONTE-CARLO
Telex: Parisotel
Telephone 018-11

June 8, 1960

Dear Folks,

I am sorry I haven't written sooner, but with the warm weather finally here there seems to be so many things to do and places to see plus classes I really haven't had a chance.

Mom, well your big day has finally come and passed. Hope you received my telegram. Really would have loved to be there for your graduation!! For a present, I am knitting you a sweater in blue. I only have the back done now. Please write and let me know all the details about the graduation.

It really feels horrible to be 21. It was much more fun to be 20 without a care in the world!

We just had a vacation for Pentecost from last Friday noon till Tuesday night. Susie, Betty, Peter, and I drove down to the Riviera in my car and most of the other girls in the apartment rented a car and we all went down. Spent my birthday in Monte Carol swimming all day. And then at night we stayed in the best hotel. Took the $10 Mom sent and spent it all on dinner. We ate on top of our hotel and had lobster, martini, French fries, wine, and strawberry cream cake for dessert. There was a band and a lovely view over the coast. It was a little expensive but I really enjoyed it! Afterwards we went to the Casino just to look around. Stayed in the beautiful hotel for two nights and spent the other two night in rat-traps. Our nice hotel had a beautiful beach complete with even a swimming pool, which we had free passes to enter! One of my friends from San Francisco knew a fellow in Monte Carlo who owns a fruit shop, so we looked him up. He turned out to be young and gay and took us to a strawberry festival back in a little mountain town. Biggest strawberries I have ever seen in my life! Then we drove all over the mountains in back of Monaco until we reached a stand that only sold cheese, bread, and wine. It was located on top of a mountain with no town nearby. There were all sorts of local people there. The place was really picturesque! Drove back Tuesday and after a 10-hour drive arrived at 12:30 A.M.

Mom and Dad, you will never believe this, but after wanting a car so long now that I have it, I don't want it. I don't even really enjoy driving now with a shift. I don't think I will ever get the shifting down pat. I received the bank draft and have had the car for about four weeks. Sister Benvenuta told me tonight I can't drive again until I leave for Oslo because I got back late last night. She thought I should be back by 8:45, which is stupid; we would miss a whole half-day or more of sun. We made up a phony excuse but she isn't understanding at all. Nannette is definitely driving to Oslo with me. But, Sister Benvenuta says you will have to write me a letter of permission to drive and send it directly to her. She is really a "witch". I am leaving here July 1st, so please try to get the letter off as soon as possible.

My boat passage home is really "messed up". I still have a reservation from Cannes, but I have decided it is really stupid to sail from there when I will be in Oslo. I definitely don't want to go back to the continent. I really want to see Berlin then perhaps leave from le Havre in France about the 23rd. It would take forever to drive all way down to Cannes. Wrote Bud and told him to get me a reservation on his ship, but I don't want it now because it lands in Montreal and I definitely want to land in New York. Went in last week to American

Express in Bern and explained the whole situation to the man and be said he would do what he could for me but all the ships are filled now for August sailings. Will write Mrs. Carlson tomorrow and explain the whole problem to her. Is there any why possible you can get me a reservation on a ship leaving from Le Havre about the 23rd of August? It seems it is easier to get reservations in the States because agencies buy in blocks of tickets.

I finally bought my watch and love it! The novelty of changing bands is great!! I even bought another one of green all to match my cocktail dress. Mom, if you are still planning to send me the money it is $31.00. By the way, what happened to the family crest you were going to send? If I have the ring made up here I am going to have to have the crest immediately.

Haven't heard from the University of Colorado yet, but I have sent in my re-entrance blank. Also, I haven't heard about my room for next year and I wrote before spring vacation. Should I send my trunk to Colorado or home? Susie said she will take it home on her boat the 17th of July and send it railway express from New York. This may be best if someone will have time at home to unpack it and send my clothes to the cleaners and take out all souvenirs. I have to be at school the 15th of September and I won't have much time to do this all myself coming home so late. Please let me know immediately what to do with it. Also, I don't even have a ship yet, so at least I would have some place to send it when I leave and the clothes won't get moth eaten.

One of the apartment "crew" was sent home last week for breaking a stupid rule that we all have been breaking all year, but she just happened to get caught. The fellow who lives next door is tremendous and was going out with Linda. She was going over to his apartment occasionally, nothing evil, and this is against the rules so she was sent home. She is really a wonderful girl and comes from an excellent family in the East.

Dad, thanks for sending the money to St. Olaf's. I am really happy to hear we joined Glen Oak again and am sorry I won't be home this summer to enjoy it. I think it is great you have been getting away from the office more and out playing golf. It was ridiculously high to send my films airmail so they are now on the way regular mail. Please let me know how they turn out. Will write Bob tomorrow about meeting to get the films you are sending with him for me. Dad, I have been getting the Glen Ellyn News and really enjoy reading it although it usually comes at least a month late, thanks. Don't worry about my money. I should have enough to get up to Oslo.

Mom, Dad, and Susie, really enjoyed all the birthday cards. They all came just before I left for Monaco. The birthday money was really appreciated too! Also, received Mom's graduation announcement and was really impressed.

My fraternity had their last "big fling" a couple of weeks ago. We all boarded a rented bus and drove around the countryside. Then we went to the sponsor's chalet on Lake Gruyere for cocktails. It was really nice. The chalet is situated way off the road down next to the lake. It is really peaceful there without any houses near, people or roads. His chalet is small and built so there is no upkeep, lawns, or need or paint. It is just a small new little chalet. This man seems so happy because he has this place just 15 minutes out of Fribourg where he can go on the weekends away from everything with his family. It is really too bad there aren't more places like this in the States. After this we went to another little town where they had a huge banquet table set for dinner and the whole place decorated for spring. We had a delicious dinner and then stayed and danced for the rest of the night. It was really a nice affair.

The weekend before last Susie and I went to the Passion Play at Ommeramergau in Germany. It is really a fantastic play. Just about the whole town takes part in it. They act the life of Christ from Palm Sunday until the Resurrection. The costumes and acting were excellent. In one scene there must have been at least two hundred people. The play lasts all day with a break for lunch. The stage is outside and the people inside. I took some movies in the morning. It rained in the afternoon so it was impossible to take pictures but this added atmosphere to the play. Drove there and back for $6.00 each. On the train it costs about $18.00. Although gas is expensive in Europe, it is much cheaper to drive then take the train.

The man at American Express called the Holland American Line and Sister George hasn't canceled my reservation yet. I told Sister Benvenuta I didn't want it week ago. It might help if you called her and tell her to cancel it or change it to the Statendam on the 24th of August. I can't possibly leave the 17th of July as originally planned now that I am going to Oslo.

I have enjoyed reading all the mail from home. Glad to see everything seems to be running smoothly. Hope to hear from you all soon...

P.S. Don't forget:

1. Letter to Sister Benvenuta about driving to Oslo.
2. Call Sister George about my ticket for July 17th.
3. Sending me the family crest and money for the watch.

Love,
Romayne

Photo of Patty Belton and myself in Egypt by the Pyramids enclosed.

GOLDEN CIRCLE SERVICE
on board aircraft
(Stationery)

Dear Folks,

Received a letter from Bob telling me about canceling his car. I suggested he buy a EURAILPASS for $125 that last for 2 months first class travel on all European trains. He and Bud could really save a lot of money if they each had one. However, you can only buy them in the States from a travel agent. Just wrote Bob and Bud express explaining the situation at their port in Southampton. If they want the passes, I told them to wire you to purchase them and send them to American Express in London immediately. If you receive a wire from them you can buy the passes at a travel agency and they will save money. All the fellows over here travel that way during long vacations.

Since I received Mom's letter first, I will answer it first. Your graduation party sounded wonderful. I think I was more surprised than you when I received your letter. I wrote Mrs. Carlson explaining my passage home. Tell Dad not to worry about the credit card. It won't work in Europe anyway even if it says international on it. I have already inquired and they have never heard of credit cards over here. Does this mean I no longer have any life insurance? Sending the check back endorsed. I wrote a note to your friend Joyce Berckman in Paris offering to help if I could and telling her perhaps I would be in Paris before sailing home.

Dad, thanks for all the info. Got a note from Bob saying he doesn't have any films for me. However, he is calling the 30th of June. I will probably see him on the way up to Oslo. You're an angel to take care of all my clothes in my trunk. Will send the key in the next letter. I started working on sending the car home. Called today and the man will let me know before I leave the ship. Asked him about sending it directly to Chicago. He is looking into it for me. There doesn't seem to be much of a problem. Thanks for sending the check for the watch for Christmas.

Checked today about having the rings made. Tomorrow she is going to have a large selection for me to choose the style. They should be finished just before I leave. There isn't enough time to get your ring size so I will be sure to get something large enough. You can always have it made smaller. Will let you know the price within the next few days. Sister Benvenuta received your letter and all is okay on that front. Thanks.

Things are coming to an end here. It is really sad. I have my truck packed already. Next week I have to take my exams a week early, so I can get to Oslo on time. It is really a mess getting it all arranged.

Last Thursday for the feast of Corpus Christi we got off school. They had a two-hour procession. It was really impressive. Everyone just about in the town marched in it from the tiniest children, my friend Rosette, the fraternities, Swiss guards, to the professors. They had four altars set up outside. The priest stopped the parade four times to give benediction. At this time everyone in the town was still. The cannon went off and the people kneeled in the streets, then the cannon went off again to signal the end.

Rosette

Saturday a fellow I met in Zurich who only speaks Italian came down to see me. We went swimming, out to dinner, and then dancing. Actually Italian and French languages are similar. All I had to do was add a few a, e, and o's to the end of words! Would really like to learn Italian next. Also, have been going out with a Swiss Italian from Lugano who is studying here. However, he had to leave last week to go in the army.

Have got eight hours of classes tomorrow, so I must close now and get to work. The end is coming too soon. Will write again next week about the rings and boat developments. Hope you can help out Bud and Bob if they wire and you send their passes right away. I don't think there is any trouble getting them. Also, if there is not enough time to send them to England, Bob said they were going to Holland perhaps he will request that they be sent there. They are really a good deal!

Love to all, Romayne

P.S. Karen Hudson came here a few weeks ago. She is studying at the University of Vienna only for the spring semester. I gave her a bed in the apartment. Sister Benvenuta wouldn't let her stay in the Villa. Her sister is getting married in Nevada. Her folks are coming here this summer.

P.S.S. Also heard Dick Pond is married!! Dean of Elmhurst College was here last week.

HOTEL DE PARIS MONTE-CARLO
Teleg. – Parisotel Telephone 018-11

June 22, 1960

Dear Folks,

First of all, I have the rings ordered for Dad and Myself. The lady is rushing them so they will be ready a week from today when I leave. They will cost about $134.00 for both of them. Dad's is more than mine because of the quantity of the gold. Please send me the money immediately special delivery. This letter should arrive Monday morning. Mom, please call Dad at the office to send the money so I can get it by Thursday.

Our route to Oslo is in Switzerland up to Basel in Germany autobahn to Heidelberg, Hanover to Hamburg, then to Denmark. There are two routes one to Copenhagen and up the Swedish coast. The other up to the most northern point in Denmark and take a ferry boat across to Oslo. We haven't checked to see which way is best as yet. Will check road conditions, fairy times etc.

I am giving my trunk key to Susie Herkes who is taking my trunk home. She will need it to go through customs in New York. She lives in Riverside so she can mail or drop off the key at our house. I do have an extra key. If you think it is better I will send it to you. The driving in Switzerland shouldn't be bad. Most of the high mountains are in the South.

What would you think if I would go to the American University in Beirut, Lebanon. I could get a degree there next year. It would solve all my boat problems. A degree from there would really mean something. The university there is run exactly like the universities in the States.

Things are really coming to an end here. Have got my exams lined up now almost. Really hate to leave here. I have a lot of friends now.

Got class now.....
Love, Romayne

Back of Hotel de Paris envelop with Glen Ellyn, Illinois postmark June 25, 1960 and following note: Hope Bob and Bud got their rail passes.

Chapter 8

Life at the University of Oslo Summer School

July 2, 1960

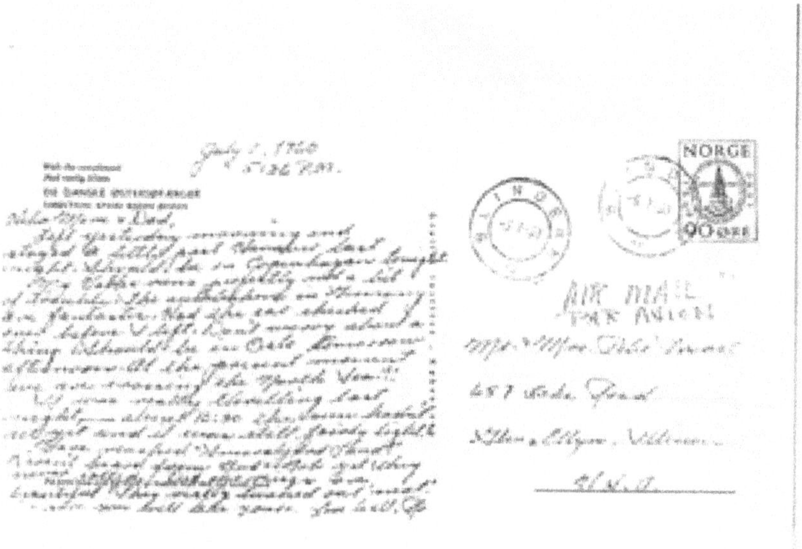
NORGE
90 ØRE
AIR MAIL
PAR AVION

Note on back of Post Card of Danish Ferry Boat
Postmarked July 6, 1960

Hello Mom and Dad,

Left yesterday morning and stayed a little past Hanover last night. Should be in Copenhagen tonight.

My Volks runs perfectly not a bit of trouble. The autobahns in Germany are fantastic. Had the car checked over before I left. Don't worry about a thing. Should be in Oslo tomorrow afternoon. At the present moment we are crossing the North Sea!

It was really thrilling last night---about 10:30 the sun hadn't set yet and it was still fairly light. Have reached "Smorsbjord Land". Haven't heard from Bud or Bob yet. They never called.

Dad our rings are beautiful! They really turned out "neat". I'm sure you will like yours.

Love to all, Ro

Handwritten on an Aerogramme

Postmarked Blindern, Norge

(Father wrote July 5, 1960 on front. He most always wrote date on envelope.)

July 5, 1960

Dear Mom and Dad,

Arrived Sunday morning about 3 am. We had a nice trip up here. After I wrote you the post card, we stayed in Copenhagen that night. Went to the Tivoli Gardens that is a huge amusement park with a little lake, cafes, all sorts of stands and rides. It is a beautiful place. The next morning I made a supreme effort to get to church. The lady at our pension told me of a convent only "5 minutes" away where they had masses. After 20 minutes I found the convent but they didn't have masses! Pow! Went back jumped in the car and found what I thought, and the lady outside said, was a Catholic Church. Well, they didn't have kneelers but every lady had a hat on and the priest came out investments. However, after 40 minutes the priest changed into a black robe. I noticed in the back of the songbook something about Martin Luther so I decided this wasn't a Catholic mass. But, it was too late to find another one. It was a cute Danish church!!

Before we left went sightseeing around Copenhagen a little. Saw the famous Mermaid Statue by Jacobson. It is very well done. It is located on a rock just off the shore in a beautiful park. It looks like a real mermaid who just decided to sit on the rock for a while. Also, saw the changing of the guard.

Met some Norwegian fellows on the ferry between Norway and Sweden! It rained all the way through Sweden. But, we stopped many times for coffee, rolls, and a big dinner of Swedish meatballs with our friends.

The American Embassy had a nice lawn party the 4th of July for the Americans. The ambassador here is a woman! She's about 50 and supposedly really "sharp". I have decided I want to be ambassador to Italy!!! Met a fellow who took me out later to a real nice nightclub on the end of a pier – excellent calypso music.

Oslo is nice, but I miss Switzerland. I really loved it there. It is so blasé to speak English all the time. I have decided the charm of Europe is in the languages! It is the thing that adds the mystery and the sparkle to the people.

However, I am very excited because about a month ago I decided on a new plan for the U. S. and here in Norway they are already following it. I am really excited this is successful because everyone laughed at me. I decided that people in the States should only eat two meals a day.

This would save a lot of wasted time. The wife could concentrate on only one good meal and not be a "kitchen slave". And, the husband and wife and children could spend more time together.

If anyone wanted to go out in the evening they would have more time to get ready! Besides, you would appreciate eating more. Here in Norway people work from 8 -4. They have a big breakfast maybe take out 15 minutes for lunch and eat a sandwich at the desk, and then get home at 4:15 for a huge meal. It is really thrilling to think my "radical" idea is already being practiced!

I have a reservation home on the Queen Mary of Cunard Line leaving Cherbourg, France, August 25th tourist class, for $243.50. In case I come home I better take it. Dad, I have to have the money

in immediately. I already put a $30 deposit down on it. Have you received the money from my other reservation as yet? I told an Italian American friend married to a Swiss gal the day before we left and somehow he got this for me!! I am probably one of the luckiest people in the world, perhaps someday I will do something to pay back for all the good fortune I have. Please send a check for $2.20 (in case Swiss francs are low) immediately directly to:
Pavoni, Aubert & Co. S.A. Place de la Gare 38 Fribourg, Suisse
Nino said he would take care of it from there and send me the ticket.

Thanks, Dad.

Classes are fairly interesting. I'm taking International Relations, Social and Political Institutions, and Norwegian Economic Life and Problems. The economic course is excellent. The professor changes about every three days. The Profs are men from parliament, bank owners, minister of foreign affairs and men of this character.

Have also made friends with an Irish Philosophy teacher, who teaches existentialism in the States. He is going to give me a quick two-week course in it. I am not really "crazy" about Scandinavia like I'm about Southern Europe yet.

I'm checking into the American University in Beirut. Will discuss it again after I find out the results.

Love my car now. No more problems shifting. It just runs, no trouble at all, and never stops.

You don't have a thing to worry about.

Dying to see Bud and Bob but haven't heard from them as yet. Sorry Dick isn't here. Susie still waiting to hear from you. Frank, if your girlfriend wants, I will write her a recommendation for Alpha Chi Omega. Let me know. If so you will have to write and tell me about her and her activities and qualities.

Mom, I don't want you to think I don't like my home just because I want to finish school here because I love it. I would like to come home but there are wonderful opportunities here. We can discuss this later when I hear some results, "Political Scientist".

They have beautiful Norwegian ski sweaters for only $15.00 hand knitted if anyone's interested let me know. In the States I have priced them and they sell for at least $30.00.

Dad, I don't need any money immediately, but I will shortly. Don't know exactly how much. I think $75.00 or $100.00 will be plenty. Haven't exactly figured out how much for the car yet. Shipping schedules aren't all set as yet. Will have no trouble shipping it directly to Chicago.

Love to all, Romayne

P. S. You can buy these air letters for about 10 cents in the States. Write soon.

AEROGRAMME
Written on outside of Aerogramme: "Forgot! I'm also auditing a course in Elementary Norwegian language for no credit!"
July 25, 1960
Monday

Dear Mom and Dad,

Business first—Dad, you have really put me in a very embarrassing position by paying for my ticket in such a manner. The travel agency in Switzerland is angry with my friend and me because now they don't get their commission. As you know, reservations are very had to obtain and they could have sold it to anyone else immediately, but since my friend was a good friend they gave it to him as a personal favor. Dad, I really wish you had more faith in my friends and me. I'm a better judge of people to have swindlers and cheats as friends. Besides you can always cancel a check. I faithfully promised to send the money immediately to him. I still don't understand what the check for $2.20 is for when I paid $30.and you paid $237. I don't understand also how I can get $19.50 back as you said when my ticket costs $243.50. The travel agency you dealt with must really be money hungry when they know they are taking someone else's commission. I appreciate your sending the money but if in doubt send it straight to me please.

Next, as I said before Sister Benvenuta is a "witch". She has a habit of writing nasty letters home to folks. Definitely do not pay her. I am planning to write her tomorrow. First of all it is impossible to have deep scratches and cigarette burns on glass topped dresser and Formica topped desk and straw chair and bed with no wood. Regarding wallpaper, there were no grease spots by my bed. The only spot on the wall was there when we moved in and it is probably because of the pipes there. We did have a few small straight pinholes but we had permission to use pins on the walls to put things up. Broken glass did not exist. The glass from the "new nightstand" broke when it was being carried over from the "old basement". The other nightstand never had any glass.

I sincerely wish Frank wouldn't come to New York to meet me if he is going to fight with Susie all the time per usual. If my reservation goes through, now that it is completely messed up, I shall arrive Tuesday, August 30 PM. Car shipment is also messed up at present, but directly to Chicago. If you want, I can change it to New York and save money on transportation home. If not, please make a train reservation for me Sunday, September 4th. For hotel reservations, get me college rates much cheaper. You might save money getting them for Frank too. They never check to see if one of us is in college. The Biltmore gives them about $5.00 a night. Think the Sheraton also for about $3.00 a night. Really excited you are all coming to meet me!!!

I have been accepted back at the University of Colorado but not my credits as yet. Wrote my sorority housemother last week about a room there, since I never heard from the girl I wrote about this.

Don't worry about sharks. I will be careful. There were many danger areas in San Francisco last summer because of this.

Summer school here is excellent. I am really learning a lot. Professors are tops. Most powerful man in the labor party spoke last week.

After midterm exams had a four-day break and drove to Stockholm! Interesting city – had lots of fun. They have a fantastic outdoor museum there with buildings from the 17th century.

King gave us a garden party. We were all presented to him!! I got to

talk to him. Thrilling!
Didn't rain.

Moroccan Embassy had a party for a limited number. Nannette and I got to go because we speak French. Ambassador seems like a real "good Joe". Nice party!

Has been raining every day since I arrived. Last Friday was the first sunny day. Went sailing yesterday in the Oslo Fjord. Social life was the only thing not hurt by the rain.

Mom, Dad, and Susie glad to receive your letters. Am really happy things at home seen to be going so smoothly. Hope everything keeps on like this. Please let me know what you think of Mrs. De la Croix.

See you soon. Love Ro

Written on the outside of the Aerogramme: Not auditing Norwegian anymore—too much work for summer time. WRITE

Saturday 8-8-60

Dear Mom and Dad,

Everything has been worked out nicely so far. Please send the enclosed letter to Ellen Downs (address in letter) with a $25.00 room deposit for next year.

I have not heard as yet from American Express in Switz; therefore, I am sending my car to New York on the Hamburg-American Line. Complete change for delivery and insurance will be $151.00. I would appreciate it if you could send this soon as possible so I could finish this matter. The car will arrive in New York August 31st. Mom please pack light. My trunk will only hold a small suitcase not regular size. Please for you, Frank, and Susie bring as a maximum two "weekend" cases and dresses and suits in a dress bag (not your green fold-up case.) I will send my large suitcase home on Bud and Bob's ship and have them bring it home from Montreal. Are they still leaving August 23rd on the SS Homeric from LeHarve as originally planned?

Received my ticket for the Queen Mary yesterday. They took out about $5.00 for cost of cancellation etc. Dad, you were really sweet to send me their commission. However, since they took out this money I don't think it is necessary to send them the commission. Instead for my friend and his wife I will send them some Norwegian hand knitted booties and mittens for the baby that is on the way. They are really cute and rather inexpensive. Do you want me to return your check? I should arrive in New York Tuesday PM.

Dad, the Rotary Club here is taking thirty summer school students (including me) out to their summer cottage for dinner Monday night!!

The City Hall has sent us all invitations for a party they give for the summer school Tuesday night!

Also, went to a very nice party in a Norwegian home last week. Lasted until about 4 am and the folks were home. Good music, drinks, and later scrambled eggs!

Speaking of food, the food here is terrible. Dad, you would really hate it—we have fish, fish, fish, fish, cauliflower or cabbage, and always boiled potatoes. Then for lunch we have a smorgasbord that consists of leftovers from dinner plus cheese.

Spørrelystne studenter i Stortinget

Me in Parliament

[illegible]

Received a reply from Sister Benvenuta. She is sending back your money. The only definite complaint she could make to me was the wallpaper under the desk by the door. So do not send back the money—my desk was always in front of the radiator. Will write her a note about this.

Monday

The school had a dance Sat. night and drawing. I won a prize! Book of plays by Ibsen. Last night the Italian ambassador's daughter had a small private party at the residence.

Because I know the Italian students here very well, I was invited! It was very casual held in her living room—served beer and spaghetti.

Yesterday afternoon I went sailing with a girl from Scotland, boy from Germany, and one from Austria in a boat from the Canadian embassy!

Don't know definitely my plans from Aug 12 to 25. But tentatively going to Copenhagen for a day, Hamburg couple of days while I drop off my car. Fly round trip to Berlin and then to Paris. Write me American Express, 11 Rue Scribes, Paris.

Have exams this week and must study, so you will probably not hear from me until I see you in New York Mom and Dad at home.

See you soon—Romayne

P.S. Waiting to receive my grades from Suisse. Midterm grades here B, C, and one not received as yet.

Sailing in Norway

UNIVERSITY OF OSLO

INTERNATIONAL SUMMER SCHOOL

CERTIFICATE OF ACHIEVEMENT

This is to certify that

ROMAYNE L. TROOST

by fulfilling all requirements and passing the necessary examinations, has satisfactorily completed a regular course* at the International Summer School of the University of Oslo, held from

July 2 to August 12, 1960

Rector of the University

Director of the Summer School

Oslo October, 1960

* (Six semester-hour credits with at least a C-average.)

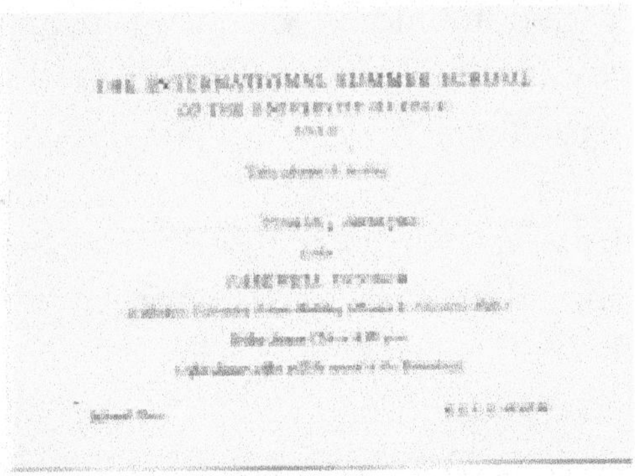

THE INTERNATIONAL SUMMER SCHOOL

FAREWELL DINNER

EPILOGUE

Upon completion of summer school in Oslo, I drove with a girl friend from my hometown to Copenhagen and Berlin (that was before the wall was erected that divided the city). In Berlin I left her and proceeded to Hamburg to ship my car to the States. Enroute to Cherbourg, France to board the Queen Mary; I hitch hiked to the ferry for Belle Isle en Mer off the coast of France to spend a few days.

The Voyage on the Queen Mary to New York brought me back home with a desire to see the entire world. The small town girl had been transformed and wanted to be "a citizen of the world". I did return to the University of Colorado where I earned a Bachelor of Arts degree. Then with my life's belongings in my green Volkswagen I moved to New York City.

Not needing a car in New York City, I sold it. And with that money I took a trip around the world by myself. The knowledge I gained by living in Europe and traveling throughout the Middle East and meeting the different people in the world, gave me the confidence to travel alone.

I met my husband in Chicago when I was planning a trip around South America. We have two daughters who we sent to Europe for their Junior Year abroad.

Eventually I did see all the continents and over 140 countries. Although I still love to travel my bucket list is empty. I feel that my life has been enriched and broadened by my travels. I would recommend to everyone to study a year abroad when you are young and impressionable. Your life will be changed forever. You will be able to read the newspaper and look through the headlines and government leaders' actions into the hearts of the people in the world. It will give you a fascination and wonder for all the peoples of the world and an appreciation of their culture. You will be part of the world and your heart will be opened to feel it.

ACKNOWLEDGMENTS

I am indebted to the following people for their help and encouragement in bringing these letters to be published in book form.

First, my friend D Clancy who read my letters and encouraged me to go further because they show the innocence of an age that no longer exists.

Second, Adrian Smith who gave me the tools to put the letters together in book form and guidance in preparing for publication.

Thanks to my readers Susie Herkes Ingallinera and Victoria Scogland who gave me valuable comments after reading my manuscript. And, Vicky's friend Ann Carpenter who encouraged me by wanting to make a movie out of my story.

I am also grateful to the International Women Associates members of the Arabic Group for their favorable response when I read my letters from the Middle East at their meetings.

I can't forget my children, Tania and Tasha, who encouraged me when I put my first draft together for the Arabic Group.

And, to my husband, Ted, who has met many of the students and foreign friends from my year abroad and embraced them all.

Big thanks to Ragdale for hosting a writer's seminar where I met Heather Buchanan, a publisher interested in my book.

APPENDIX

SPEECH: *MIDDLE EASTERN MEMORIES* (April 2005)

I did this talk about 10 years ago when I first joined the International Women Associates (IWA). Shirhara and Marileez were co-chairs of the Arab group. They asked me to do a program, I think, because I was always telling them how much I enjoy this group and my fascination with the Middle East:

> I was hesitant to do a talk because I did not think I had enough to say to you for my attitude toward the Middle East is just based on my feelings. But Shirhara convinced me that the new thinking is, "I feel therefore I am" and not "I think therefore I am" as Descartes wrote.
>
> What is it that holds me to this part of the world? First of all, let me tell you my background. I am 4th generation American with ancestors from many middle European countries. I grew up in a small town west of Chicago. My first exposure to a larger world was when I spent my junior year in college abroad in Switzerland. While I was there, we had six weeks spring break. One of our fellow students was a girl from Iran. She invited us to visit her over this break. The girls I lived with decided we should travel through the Middle East and stay with our friend in Iran only for part of the time. This was in the spring of 1960 when young girls did not go traveling alone so two of the girl's aunts came along as chaperones. I was not involved in the planning of this trip. We visited Turkey, Lebanon, Syria, Jordan, Israel, Egypt, and Greece in addition to Iran.
>
> I always wrote letters home to my parents about my experiences, which my father saved. Rereading these letters today, I think one of the main reasons I was so moved by this region was the friendliness and acceptance of us even though we were foreigners. The warmth and generosity of the Middle Eastern people was exceptional.

[Read excerpts from letters.]

These excerpts give you some idea of my experiences in the Middle East. Yet, what really holds me to it? Was it my age at the time? Yet, I chose to go back to Egypt twice since my initial visit, and Jordan and Turkey. A lot of it is just a feeling. I felt it was where the "East meets the West". I was fascinated by the differences such as everyday foods, products and way of doing things and yet did not feel alienated because of the similarities such as homes, cooking styles, and lifestyles. Whereas, when I visited the Orient I felt removed from the people because their lifestyles seemed to be entirely different from mine.

The Middle East, especially Egypt and Lebanon, has always remained dear to me because of the tremendous hospitality and uniqueness as you have just heard from my letters, such as the water pipes, bazaars, pyramids, sounds at night…It is a feeling of excitement of life being lived at the moment. It is different from my other trips because I felt part of it. Was it because of my age? My personality? Their hospitality? The uniqueness of the sights around me? The difference and yet the sameness of the Western culture? I don't know what exactly has held my emotions to this part of the world. All I can tell you is that it captured me when I was young and still fascinates me today. I was willing to do this program again today—so perhaps I can pay back in a small way the wonderful hospitality that captured me over 40 years ago.

Was my experience uniquely mine or will others experience it? I do not know. I only know that this short time of my life that I spent in the Middle East has influenced my opinions, ideas, and most of all my feelings about this part of the world. Many other countries are more predictable being of a "true" Western culture. The Middle East is truly a part of the world where the East meets West and therefore has captured my emotions and my heart.

About the Author

Romayne Kazmer is a world traveler. She attributes her love of travel and curiosity of the world to her year abroad in 1959/60 studying at the University of Fribourg in Switzerland and summer school at the University of Oslo in Norway. She traveled extensively throughout Europe and the Middle East at that time. Her two daughters also spent their junior year at universities abroad in London and Paris.

After returning home to her small town, Glen Ellyn, Illinois, she completed her studies at the University of Colorado. Then she moved to New York City with all her life's belongings. At 23, she was still fascinated by the world she had experienced and wanted to see it all. Taking a leave of absence from her job and with her life's savings, she traveled around the world alone.

She met her husband, Ted, while planning a trip around South America. They shared a love of travel and ventured forward to over 141 countries and all the continents. They live in Bannockburn, Illinois.

It is remarkable that this small town girl shares her insights and memories from the year that changed her life.

Printed in the USA
CPSIA information can be obtained
at www.ICGtesting.com
LVHW021206091223
766098LV00061B/3614

9 781735 740805